Christian Conscience and Negro Emancipation

CHRISTIAN CONSCIENCE AND NEGRO EMANCIPATION

RALPH L. MOELLERING

FORTRESS PRESS • PHILADELPHIA

Library of Congress Catalog Card Number 65-18282

UB993

Printed in U.S.A.

8273A65

To the members of all races at First Immanuel Lutheran Church and to all of my associates who shared in my 1953-58 ministry on the Near West Side of Chicago.

Preface

Conscience and emancipation are the two key concepts around which this book revolves. It expresses the belief that if the full implications of Christian convictions are understood and applied to the race question, the pace of constructive social change in our country can be accelerated.

More than a century has elapsed since slavery was abolished in the United States. The full emancipation of the Negro, however, continues to be more a hopeful vision than a completed reality. Despite the commendable progress made in the last decade, an enormous unfinished task still confronts the men and women who take social justice seriously. The Civil Rights Law of 1964, a significant step in the right direction, has not marked the end of the struggle; tensions and inequities persist in both North and South.

Especially among youthful enthusiasts, a moral fervor unsurpassed since the days of the abolitionist crusade has mobilized forces to eliminate the blight of racial discrimination from America. A growing number of people professing a Christian motivation are becoming allies of the drive for Negro freedom. Nevertheless, the Christian conscience still needs to be aroused from its prolonged slumber.

One of the most disappointing chapters in church history reveals the sanction which the institutional church has often given to slavery or the equivocal compromise with which it has blessed or tolerated its proponents. No Christian today can detach himself from the sins of his forefathers, because he is inescapably enmeshed in the social evils which have resulted from the failures and offenses of the past. Anyone who shows a lack of concern and moral courage over human rights helps by his very silence and evasiveness to prolong the agony of the exploited and to postpone the dawn of genuine emancipation.

Beyond providing an historical background for understanding the striking relationship between pre-Civil War disputations over slavery and the post-World War II controversies over segregation, this book seeks to offer an interpretation of the pivotal events in the racial crisis of the last few years. Illustrations from current fiction are used because they so vividly depict the complications involved in the explosive area of sex and interracial marriage. Contemporary literature also throws light on the reputation which the church has acquired as a consequence of its neglect and mistakes. While the book offers an historical and theological framework for examining such current problems as fair housing legislation, more practical, I would assume, are some of the specific recommendations that are set forth to make Christian social action meaningful and helpful. Stress is placed on the urgency of introducing daring initiative and imagination for a relevant ministry in the inner city.

The incentive for writing this book comes from a persistent urge to alert the church to its responsibility in assuming a more positive and more active role in overcoming racial prejudice. This concern has been nurtured and informed by academic research at Harvard University. More important, it has been sharpened by direct encounter with a diversity of social problems during a five year urban ministry in Chicago's notorious Near West Side. This personal exposure to the perils and challenges of the city jungle left an indelible imprint on my own conscience, compelling me to assert my convictions and to advance whatever counsel I can provide to hasten the day of liberation so that Negroes and whites can live together in peace and with mutual respect.

RALPH L. MOELLERING

Ash Wednesday, 1965

Contents

Acknowledgments

Thanks are due to the Lutheran Human Relations Association of America and its Executive Secretary from 1954 to 1964, Dr. Andrew Schulze, for the opportunity to serve as essayist at the workshop for professional church workers conducted on the campus of Valparaiso University during the summer of 1959, when some of the material found in this book was first presented and discussed; to my former associate in the campus ministry at Berkeley, Lois Dorow, for help in research; to my wife Clarice for typing the manuscript; and to Jo Duisman, a member of my church at the University of California, for preparing the index.

R. L. M.

Acknowledgment is made to the following for permission to quote material: Henry Regnery Company; Charles Scribner's Sons; *U. S. News and World Report;* The Association for the Study of Negro Life and History; Longmans, Green and Company; Columbia University Press; *Lutheran News;* The New American Library of World Literature; Harcourt, Brace and World; Clemonce Sabourin; Sheed and Ward; Alfred A. Knopf; Farrar, Straus and Company; *The Cresset; Christian Century; Saturday Review; Vanguard; Arena; The Lutheran Layman;* Harper and Row; The Dial Press; Harvard University Press; Grove Press; and Simon and Schuster.

1 Emancipation—When?

"Now, therefore, I, Abraham Lincoln . . . do order and declare that all persons held as slaves . . . are, and henceforth shall be, free . . ."

It was a radiant day of deliverance. Grateful Negroes assembled to give thanks to Lincoln and to God. Crowds erupted with cheers and shouting. At Tremont Temple in Boston the rapture continued unabated for two hours. After midnight the throng, led by the incomparable Negro orator Frederick Douglas, moved to the Twelfth Baptist Church and continued to sing and pray until dawn.

In his "Boston Hymn" composed on the day of emancipation, January 1, 1863, Ralph Waldo Emerson exulted:

> I break your bonds and masterships
> And I unchain the slave:
> Free be his heart and hand henceforth
> As wind and wandering wave.[1]

Abraham Lincoln became known as the Great Emancipator. An image was projected of "the kindly, careworn man sitting at his desk and, with a few strokes of the Presidential pen, striking the shackles from millions of bondsmen."[2]

[1] Quoted by Arna Bontemps, *100 Years of Negro Freedom* (New York: Dodd, Mead & Co., 1962), p. 3.
[2] Richard N. Current, "Lincoln and the Proclamation," *The Progressive,* XXVI (December, 1962), 9.

A careful examination of the circumstances leading up to the memorable event indicates that the humanitarian motive for liberating slaves was probably secondary. Winning the bloody internecine war, together with domestic politics and foreign policy, weighed heavily in bringing about "the day of days." Not until the Union had gained its decisive victory at Antietam on September 22, 1862, did President Lincoln feel free to declare his intention to end the slavery of Negroes.[3]

The record indicates that Lincoln never spoke as an abolitionist and that he feared the consequences of sudden emancipation. During the 1850's he urged that slavery be kept out of the western territories but never proposed that it be eliminated in the southern states. In his first inaugural address he still spoke of his desire to secure the rights of slaveowners to their property. Early in 1862 Lincoln proposed to Congress a plan for gradual, compensated emancipation, by state action, with federal aid. Once freed, the slaves would, with their consent, be shipped abroad. Surprising as it may seem, this "colonization" scheme of Abraham Lincoln has been cited by the extreme right wing in America as a solution for the race problem today.[4]

What these reactionaries forget is that Lincoln too was a child of his times and a product of his own environment. What is remarkable and praiseworthy is his constant growth in understanding, his deepening appreciation of the Negro's plight, and his increasing determination to give the Negro a firm place in American life. By January, 1864, he began to formulate his ideas for extending civil rights to Negroes. In his last public address on April 11, 1865, Lincoln repeated his conviction that the franchise should be

[3] A concise and definitive study of the historic document has been prepared by John Hope Franklin, *The Emancipation Proclamation* (New York: Doubleday, 1963).

[4] In protesting the Civil Rights legislation of 1964 the American Nazi Party adduced quotations from speeches by Abraham Lincoln in which he is reported to have affirmed that physical distinctions between Negroes and whites "forbid their political equality." Cf. Roy P. Basler, *Collected Works of Abraham Lincoln* (New Brunswick, N. J.: Rutgers University Press, 1953), pp. 145-46.

conferred on intelligent Negroes "and on those who serve our cause as soldiers."[5] Unfortunately these lofty intentions, including the safeguarding of liberty and opportunity for ex-slaves, lost their strongest spokesman when Lincoln was assassinated.

Long after slavery was renounced by most of the Western world, southern whites continued to hold nine-tenths of their colored people as chattel. Even before the middle of the nineteenth century the prevalent ideology in the South was an untenable anachronism. Sealed off in social and intellectual isolation, southerners, before and since the Civil War, clung with fierce desperation to dogmas which had been repudiated elsewhere. Only after a crushing defeat did slaveholders yield to emancipation.

Surrender was a traumatic experience for the South. Submission could not be averted consciously. Subconsciously and irrationally it was resisted. Reconstruction days, with all the attendant shocks of military rule, Negro enfranchisement, and social upheaval, were a bitter pill. The symbols of humiliation—federal bayonets (what hateful passions they would evoke again at Little Rock, Arkansas in 1959 and at Oxford, Mississippi, in 1962!), martial law, carpetbaggers, and restriction of southern whites—deepened their resentment. By ruse or force, as soon as they were able, adamant southerners overturned the entire enterprise. In reclaiming their own rights and privileges they again subjugated the Negro. By strategems of intimidation and with Jim Crow legislation they forced the Negro to relapse into a servile position.

Present day racial extremists have conveyed the impression that harsh policies of exclusion and proscription are an inescapable consequence of having two races in the same country with different qualities and cultural attainments. The segregation of the races, it is claimed, was always a characteristic feature of the southern way of life.

On the contrary, however, Jim Crowism is a relatively recent

[5] John Hope Franklin, "Civil Rights in American History," *The Progressive,* XXVI, 8.

development. Segregation was both unnecessary and impracticable under slavery. As long as the inferior status of the Negro was assured, white people did not find it important to avoid all physical and social contacts with him. Cooks and household servants worked closely with their masters and mistresses. White children while young were not forbidden to intermingle with colored children. For many years it was not uncommon for Negroes to be admitted to white churches, even though they might be restricted to seats in the balcony. Prior to the War between the States there was more separation of the races in the North than in the South.

For nearly two decades after the end of Reconstruction the zealots for racial ostracism were held in check. The few Negroes who had the financial means to avail themselves of good hotels or public amusements were not denied admission. The conservatives who dominated politics had inherited the attitude of plantation paternalism. For them the Negro still bore the stigma of slavery in his speech and manners and did not threaten the special privileges of the whites. They found it superfluous to humiliate him with rigidly enforced patterns of segregation. At one point the insurgent Populists of the nineties, a party of agrarian reform, tried to establish a common platform with Negroes in waging a fight against the entrenched patricians who had previously solicited, bought, or coerced Negro votes. Finding their regime in jeopardy, the conservative rulers of the South appealed to racial antipathies to unify white support. The biracial partnership of Populism began to disintegrate, and the Negroes became the scapegoat for the pent-up bitterness and frustration that accompanied the collapse of the movement. Therefore the rural South became a seed-bed for the racist propaganda of political demagogues. Jim Crow laws "kept the Negro in his place," and the signs "White" and "Colored" that marked off the dividing line were conspicuously posted in every public building.[6]

[6] For a full account of the late advent of segregation in the South, cf. C. Vann Woodward, *The Strange Career of Jim Crow* (New York: Oxford, 1957).

Meanwhile the United States Supreme Court was engaged in a policy of reconciliation between state and federal jurisdiction at the expense of the Negro. The national government was blocked in its efforts to intervene in southern states to defend Negroes. To all intents and purposes the Fourteenth and Fifteenth Amendments were nullified in their relation to the freedmen. Two decisions handed down by the high court especially paved the way for the curtailment of Negro rights and a full-blown system of segregation. In *Plessy vs. Ferguson* in 1896 the "separate but equal" doctrine was formulated which remained the law of the land until the revolutionary desegregation ruling of 1954. Then, in 1898, in the case of *Williams vs. Mississippi,* the Supreme Court provided the legal backing for disfranchisement by sanctioning the Mississippi plan for depriving Negroes of their vote.

A temporary settlement in America's racial crisis was reached as the Negro found it impossible to resist the adverse turn of events. Booker T. Washington made his "Atlanta Compromise"[7] and became the almost unrivaled leader of American Negroes until his death in 1915. Negro opinion ceased to be a deterrent to white aggression. Paradoxically the progressive movement coincided with a high wave of racism. Woodrow Wilson's promise of a "New Freedom" in the campaign of 1912 sounded attractive enough to draw many Negro votes away from the Republican party. But the first Congress in the new Democratic administration received a flood of votes proposing discriminatory legislation. Although most of the bills failed to pass, Wilson, by executive order, segregated most of the Negro federal employees in eating and rest room facilities.[8]

In the years following World War I the bane of race baiting, spawned in the South, surged through the North and West. Race

[7] Washington's intentions no doubt were good, but in proposing that Negroes retire from the political arena and be content to assume a humble industrial role he conveyed an impression of submissiveness.

[8] John Hope Franklin, *From Slavery to Freedom* (New York: Knopf, 1963), pp. 445-46.

riots and lynchings became a national disgrace. The hatred of the Ku Klux Klan reached its crest in the twenties. During the thirties racial tension eased perceptibly as the New Deal registered modest economic gains for the Negro. All the while, the wall of segregation remained impregnable. In the forties, however, a barrage of agitation and an avalanche of demands began to descend on the South from above the Mason-Dixon line. And in the large cities of the North, to which cheap Negro labor had been lured during the two World Wars, dissatisfaction was mounting over the confinement of Negroes to their ghettoes. Once again the cry for freedom was heard across the land. By the mid-fifties a "new" generation of Negroes was in full revolt, and a resensitized Christian conscience was astir.

Appropriately enough, the centennial observance of the emancipation proclamation was marked by the inauguration of a new crusade to liberate the Negro American. In 1863 slavery was officially abolished by an executive order of the President of the United States. In 1963, a hundred years later, the descendants of the slaves demanded, with more determination and persistence than they had ever displayed before, everything which emancipation in the fullest sense should imply—equality of opportunity and unrestricted freedom.

The centennial of the Emancipation Proclamation was more eventful than anyone could have predicted. It witnessed the full outburst of the Negro revolt. Hope and tragedy were intermingled in the startling rapidity with which the Negro clamor for justice rose to a mighty crescendo all over the land. Heroic actions were coupled with ugly incidents. The news media were crammed with stories about sit-ins, protest demonstrations, jailings, and riots. Even the all-white remotest hamlet in rural Iowa or northern New England became aware of the fact that America had a race problem.

The memorable year began with an unprecedented National Conference on Religion and Race, drawing together delegates from seventy participating organizations, and representing Roman Catholics, Protestants, Orthodox, and Jews. Major addresses, subsequently published,[9] were delivered by prominent priests, ministers, and rabbis. Emanating from the assembly was "An Appeal to the Conscience of the American People" which included these statements:

> Racism is our most serious domestic evil. We must eradicate it with all diligence and speed. . . . We Americans of all religious faiths have been slow to recognize that racial discrimination and segregation are an insult to God, the Giver of human dignity and human rights. . . . With few exceptions we have evaded the mandates and rejected the promises of the faiths we represent. We repent our failures and ask the forgiveness of God.[10]

In 1956 the case of Miss Autherine Lucy, who was first admitted to the University of Alabama and then expelled under the pressure of angry threats, sent a wave of admiration and trepidation down the spine of the nation. Another crisis was precipitated in 1957 when Governor Orval Faubus of Arkansas defied the federal government by calling out troops to prevent the integration of Central High School in Little Rock. America's reputation abroad was badly tarnished by the spectacle of nine Negro children being kept out of school at bayonet point.

Far worse was the violent explosion that came in the fall of 1962 when James Meredith became the first Negro to seek admission at "Ole Miss." Ross Barnett, Governor of Mississippi, insolently scorned the pleas of President Kennedy, and armed might had to be used to compel compliance with the rulings of the courts. In a night of infamy a pitched battle was fought with the backing of ex-General Edwin Walker. A British correspondent was killed as students and churchgoing towns-people joined the craze-filled rabble in hurling bricks and destroying property. Our prestige overseas descended to an all-time low as African and Asian delegates

[9] Matthew Ahmann (ed.), *Race: Challenge to Religion* (Chicago: Regnery, 1963).
[10] *Ibid.*, pp. 171-72.

to the United Nations inquired why a democracy-professing people needed armed federal agents to escort a Negro student from classroom to dormitory to dining hall at a state university.

As the centennial year began, James Meredith was still protected by armed surveillance at Oxford, Mississippi. More efforts were being planned to "crack open" the strongholds of segregation in the South. On March 18 Governor Barnett addressed the Rotary Club in Fort Wayne, Indiana. About thirty pre-theological students from Concordia Senior College picketed the meeting, protesting the Governor's actions in the Meredith case, but also deploring the hypocrisy of northern cities.[11] Even hitherto quiescent Lutherans were being aroused from their apathy and induced to share in the civil rights movement.

In the spring of 1963 the Reverend Martin Luther King, Jr. and his supporters decided to "move in" on what they regarded as the most segregated large city in the United States. White Birmingham bristled with indignation as the Negroes began their boycotts and demonstrations. As before in other places, hymns were sung and inspirational addresses were delivered in the churches. Negro spirituals like "Go Down Moses" and other songs were adapted to express the conviction that right will ultimately triumph:

> O Freedom . . . over me, and before I be a slave I'll be buried in my grave and go home to my Lord and be free. . . . I shall not be moved . . . just like a tree is planted by the water I shall not be moved. . . . We shall overcome some day. . . . Oh, deep in my heart I do believe we shall overcome some day.[12]

The home of Dr. King's brother was bombed. Young children withdrew from school to parade with placards. Spontaneous sympathy marches were conducted in Chicago, New York City, and throughout the North. But the white supremacists of Birmingham

[11] Cf. *Journal-Gazette* (Fort Wayne), March 19, 1963.

[12] See "7 Songs to Freedom" compiled and transcribed by Merritt Hedgman and S. Coleridge Huey, published privately for the Washington Assembly.

were adamant. The Ku Klux Klan burned crosses on the lawns of whites suspected of being on the verge of making concessions. "Bull" Connor resorted to police dogs and other forms of intimidation to squelch the Negro uprising. (Communists were quick to capture the propaganda value of this incident. As a tourist in Moscow in the summer of 1963 I saw the Soviet press feature the picture of a police dog tearing into the flesh of a Negro.)

All the sacrifices in time, money, and heroism yielded only minor gains in Birmingham, but the Negro revolt spread like a contagion to places in the South where Jim Crowism had never been challenged before. In Jackson, Mississippi, a citadel of last-ditch segregation, an ex-policeman was applauded as he mauled and kicked a fallen Negro. A jet of mustard was fired by a bouffant blonde at a Negro coed sitting at a dime store lunch counter. While police stood by for two riotous hours, howling white toughs splattered and cuffed impassive Negroes. From the infuriated crowd came the battle cries: "Kill the black bastards! . . . Go get 'em![13] Negroes were herded off to jail in droves. Epithets were hurled at demonstrators. Women and children were spat upon. In a test of endurance the non-violent crusaders were often manhandled and tormented. The white man was disgraced further with the slaying of NAACP organizer Medgar Evers in Jackson, Mississippi. President Kennedy declared that he was nauseated by this cowardly deed, and self-respecting southerners bemoaned the shame that had descended upon their beloved Dixie.

By way of contrast the nation could be proud of its behavior during the gigantic march on Washington late in August for "jobs and freedom." The right of disgruntled citizens "peaceably to assemble and petition" for a redress of their grievances was honorably and magnificently discharged as thousands upon thousands of Negroes and their white allies converged on the nation's capital displaying admirable restraint and self-discipline. The "Big Six" Negro organizations were reinforced by Walter Reuther's United Auto

[13] Cf. *Newsweek* (June 10, 1963).

Workers and representatives of most religious faiths. From all across the country they came, in twos, scores, and hundreds, in cars and buses and trains and chartered jets. After a rendezvous at the Washington Monument, punctuated with hymns and prayers, the orderly throng marched down Independence Avenue to the Lincoln Memorial a mile distant. As the procession advanced, there was a continual outburst of singing, cheering, and heart-warming speeches. Marian Anderson brought tears to the eyes of many as she gave an inimitable rendition of "He's Got the Whole World in His Hand." Hope was kindled anew. No miracle resulted on Capitol Hill, but a profound impression was made on millions of TV viewers. In addition, moral pressure was exerted on the Congress and the administration to act more decisively in behalf of civil rights.

Then another jolt and retrogression. Birmingham again shamed the nation in September when a Baptist Sunday school was dynamited and four Negro children were decapitated or mutilated beyond recognition in the blast. The sight of a gutted church, blood-spattered kindergarten leaflets, and grief-stricken mothers sent a shock wave of horror and outrage throughout the land. The same day a policeman shotgunned a fleeing Negro; and two Eagle scouts, after attending a segregation rally, inexplicably murdered a Negro youth. Defiance of law and order had yielded its bitter fruit.

Remorse was immediate and sincere enough; but it took a courageous young lawyer in Birmingham to pinpoint the spot where the responsibility lay. Charles Morgan, Jr., in an address before the local Young Men's Business Club, asked: "Who threw that bomb?" and supplied the self-incriminating answer: "We all did it." Conscience-stricken and exasperated over the self-righteousness of his fellow-southerners he confessed their collective culpability:

> . . . all across Alabama an angry, guilty people cry out their mocking shouts of indignity, and they say they wonder 'why?' and 'who?'. . . . The 'who' is every little individual who talks about the 'niggers' and spreads the seeds of his hate. . . . The 'who' is the jokester, the crude oaf whose racial jokes rock the party with laughter. . . . The 'who'

is all the Christians and all their ministers who spoke too late in anguished cries against the violence. The 'who' is the coward in each of us who ducks admonitions. . . .

Who is really guilty? Each of us. Each citizen who has not consciously attempted to bring about peaceful compliance with the decisions of the Supreme Court of the United States . . . each citizen who votes for the candidate who hoists the bloody flag . . . every school board member and school teacher and principal and businessman and judge and lawyer who has corrupted the minds of our youth . . . is at least as guilty, or more so, than the demented fool who threw that bomb. . . .[14]

President John F. Kennedy had met with his advisers, spokesmen for the churches, and Negro leaders throughout the anxiety-ridden centennial year. Robert Kennedy, the Attorney General, had to use federal agents to investigate crimes against Negroes, and federal power to negate the interference of Governor Wallace with integration at the University of Alabama. Prepared to forfeit the "Solid South" and risking the loss of white votes in the North in the next national election the President urged the passage of more civil rights legislation. Negroes complained about the compromises that were introduced to conform with political realities, but generally they esteemed Mr. Kennedy as their greatest benefactor in the White House since Abraham Lincoln.

Like Lincoln, Kennedy met with an untimely death at a crucial juncture in the history of the United States. As the centennial observance of the Emancipation Proclamation drew to a close, a shot was fired in Dallas, Texas that pierced the throat of the young president and sent the nation into mourning.

Two days later (November 24), under the shadow of this tragedy, the St. Louis Conference on Religion and Race conducted a procession and assembly (in which the writer participated) to visually demonstrate the concern of the churches for improved human

[14] Charles Morgan, Jr., "Who is Guilty in Birmingham," ***Christian Century*** (October 2, 1963), pp. 1195-96. Cf. Charles Morgan, Jr., *A Time to Speak* (New York: Harper, 1964).

relations in Missouri. With the endorsement of the Metropolitan Church Federation, the Archdiocese of St. Louis, and the St. Louis Rabbinical Association, a crowd estimated at 35,000 gathered near the Soldier's Memorial to walk in quiet solemnity to the Old Courthouse on the riverfront where the notorious Dred Scott decision had once been rendered. Still grieving over the incredible assassination the sober multitude augmented by a national television audience heard a Jesuit professor of law, a Jewish rabbi, and a Negro Baptist plead for an outpouring of racial justice and harmony as a fitting memorial to their deceased president.

The Christmas refrain of "Peace on earth, good will among men" was heard at the end of 1963 by a people who had experienced the greatest upheaval in race relations since the manumission of the slaves. As the New Year of 1964 dawned, and the centennial celebration itself was history, some of the most poignant questions for seers to ponder were: Can the Negro revolt which captured the limelight and reached its height during 1963 long endure? Can it remain non-violent? What new forms will it assume? Will individual Christians and the church as a whole move into the vanguard of the crusade for human freedom and dignity?

Seventy years after Abraham Lincoln drafted the Emancipation Proclamation, and thirty years before the new drive for emancipation was launched, the social prophet, Reinhold Niebuhr, offered a remarkable analysis of the impotence of the Negro American. With keen perception the author of *Moral Man and Immoral Society* diagnosed the Negro's disability in terms which have become commonplace in the 1960's but were rarely expressed during the thirties. With his usual clarity Niebuhr pierced through the illusions and assumptions of pious Christians. "Trusting in the moral sense of the white race," he realized, will never extricate the Negro from his inferior status. Violent rebellion would be equally futile. Niebuhr almost seemed to be forecasting the days of Martin Luther King when he estimated that a strategy of non-violence, such as Gandhi had resorted to in India, would be most effective for a minority which could not mobilize enough power to cope with its oppressors. Without denying that "moral and rational forces" may contribute to the improvement of relations between whites and Negroes, Niebuhr insisted that philanthropy and education were insufficient means for removing the obstacles to Negro self-realization. Nothing could substitute for "a frontal attack upon the social injustices from which the Negro suffers." Race commissions were handicapped because they were dependent largely upon voluntary concessions from the white community for the removal of objectionable practices. "Minimum rights" such as more police protection and better sanitation might conceivably be granted, but little was accomplished in overcoming "political disfranchisement" and "economic disinheritance." Even though some individuals might be prepared to accord the descendants of slaves full citizenship, the white race as a whole "will not admit the Negro to full rights if it is not forced to do so."[15]

Here one finds in the observations of a far-sighted theologian, three decades in advance, many of the underlying premises upon which the current Negro revolt is grounded. Niebuhr went on to discuss some of the specific techniques of non-violence which might cause the opposition to yield:

> Boycotts against banks which discriminate against Negroes in granting credit, against stores which refuse to employ Negroes while serving Negro trade, and against public service corporations which practice racial discrimination, would undoubtedly be crowned with some measure of success. Non-payment of taxes against states which spend on the education of Negro children only a fraction of the amount spent on white children, might be an equally efficacious weapon.[16]

If the Negro "uprising" in the sixties is not utilizing all of these devices in the particular manner prescribed, it is certainly using means which are strikingly familiar.

[15] Reinhold Niebuhr, *Moral Man and Immoral Society* (New York: Charles Scribner's Sons, 1932), pp. 252, 253. [16] *Ibid.*, p. 254.

Niebuhr likewise foresaw the ability of the Negro to exercise self-restraint under duress and withstand the provocations of white agitators:

> One waits for such a campaign with all the more reason and hope because the peculiar spiritual gifts of the Negro endow him with the capacity to conduct it successfully. He would need only to fuse the aggressiveness of the new and young Negro with the patience and forbearance of the old Negro, to rob the former of its vindictiveness and the latter of its lethargy.[17]

The date usually accepted as marking the beginning of the Negro revolt is December 1, 1955, when a tired Negro widow said "no" to the bus driver who ordered her to surrender her seat to a white man. The Montgomery bus boycott which followed became the first major instance of unyielding Negro resistance to an entrenched form of segregation. Whites who had long held to the illusion that Negroes were content with their lot were appalled to find their maids and gardeners responding to the appeal for Negro solidarity. In a laudable display of fortitude and persistence Negroes walked to work, shut their ears to taunting jeers, and pooled their resources to "hold out" until victory was attained.

Emerging as the successful exponent of non-violence and the symbolical leader of the Negro cause was the Reverend Martin Luther King, Jr., a Baptist preacher and admirer of Gandhi. "Martin," in the appraisal of Louis Lomax, "is to the Negro revolt as Paul was to the early Church; not only does he go from town to town inspiring Negroes to take action, but he returns to suffer with them in the time of trouble."[18]

Dr. King is the head of the Southern Christian Leadership Conference which was grounded on the assumption that some clergymen in southern cities were ready to use their prestige in behalf of

[17] *Ibid.*

[18] Louis Lomax, *The Negro Revolt* (New York: Signet, 1963), p. 103.

civil rights in their communities. Indeed, Negro clergymen have gone far to redeem the Christian name from the contempt it has endured through the vacillation, if not bigotry, of many white church leaders. Names like the Reverend Fred Shuttlesworth and the Reverend Ralph Abernathy immediately come to mind. Undaunted by threats of reprisals they have stood at the side of Martin Luther King and bolstered the morale of their people. Under such courageous leadership the SCLC has conducted voter registration drives, served as a coordinating center for freedom riders, and provided courses in citizenship training for illiterate and deprived Negroes.

By the time the centennial of the Emancipation Proclamation rolled around the "granddaddy" of the civil rights movement had already been in existence for fifty-four years. The National Association for the Advancement of Colored People has drawn its membership from upper-class Negroes and liberal whites. Its immediate antecedent was the Niagara movement of 1905 led by W. E. B. DuBois who was disgruntled with Booker T. Washington's conciliatory gestures and acquiescence to white domination. The NAACP drafted a platform which exposed the "naked nastiness" of "the new American creed" which warned: "fear to let black men even try to rise lest they become equals of the white." And then DuBois and his followers remonstrated: "this is the land that professes to follow Jesus Christ. The blasphemy of such a course is only matched by its cowardice."[19]

DuBois and his supporters were considered too radical until 1908, when a bloody race riot struck Springfield, Illinois. Chagrined over this episode, distinguished white northerners like Jane Addams, William Dean Howells, and John Dewey invited the militant Negroes of the Niagara movement to join them in the formation of what in 1910 became the NAACP. The announced goals of the organization were: (1) abolition of enforced segregation; (2) equal educational advantage for colored and white; (3) en-

[19] *Ibid.*, p. 117.

franchisement for the Negro; and (4) enforcement of the Fourteenth and Fifteenth Amendments of the United States Constitution.

The NAACP has always leaned heavily upon legal procedures as means for social advance. Three important court decisions in favor of its pleas came quite early. In 1915 the Supreme Court renounced the "grandfather" clauses[20] that had kept Negroes from voting in several states; in 1917 the court declared null and void a municipal ordinance compelling Negroes to live in restricted parts of town; and in 1923 the court overruled a murder conviction against a Negro, partly because Negroes had been excluded from the jury which rendered the verdict. During the decade of the forties the NAACP gained further prestige by breaking down restrictive housing covenants and by supporting Negro labor unionists. By 1962 the National Association for the Advancement of Colored People was recognized as an efficient operation, wielding stupendous influence in promoting civil rights, and with 471,060 members scattered through 1,494 branches in 48 states. Its general fund income for 1961 exceeded one million dollars.[21] To avoid confusion it should be understood that the NAACP Legal Defense and Education Fund, long administered by Thurgood Marshall, and which finances cases seeking legal redress, has been separated since 1955 from the NAACP itself. The NAACP maintains a lobby in Washington and is not tax exempt like its offspring.

In recent years the NAACP has been troubled by dissension within and reproach from without. Not everyone agrees that school desegregation should have been the focal point for a civil rights policy. Louis Lomax faults the organization for neglecting "to launch a program whose visible goals capture the imagination of the Negro masses." People on the local level, he complains, have

[20] Exemption from property-owning, tax-paying, or educational requirements in state suffrage laws was granted to those who had the right to vote on January 1, 1867, and to their lineal descendants. The clause was adopted in South Carolina (1895), Louisiana (1898), North Carolina (1900), Alabama (1901), Virginia (1902), Georgia (1908), and Oklahoma (1910).

[21] Lomax, *op. cit.*, pp. 118-22.

not been sufficiently involved in the undertakings of the NAACP.[22]

The Urban League, formed two years after the NAACP, was primarily concerned with helping Negro migrants adjust to life in the big cities, especially by finding them jobs. It has been criticized by some Negroes in the past for remaining aloof from the disputes between capital and labor. Now, under the dynamic leadership of young Whitney Young it proposes to certify the Negro masses as an underdeveloped people who need special treatment and training to prepare them for greater responsibility as they are elevated in the economic and social spheres. The high Negro crime rate, attributable in large measure to frustration and unemployment, has become a serious concern of the National Urban League.[23]

Negro laborers were long barred from white labor unions. In 1925 A. Philip Randolph organized the Pullman Porters, and by 1937 he gained full recognition and bargaining power. The Brotherhood of Sleeping Car Porters became the third member of the original Big Three, together with the NAACP and the Urban League, that pressed forward in promoting the Negro cause.

In the meantime the social upheaval of the last few years that calls for faster action and immediate results has given birth to fresh ideas and more militant organizations. A second major battle, following the clergy-directed bus boycott in Montgomery, erupted on February 1, 1960. Four Freshman from the all-Negro Agricultural and Technical College at Greensboro, North Carolina, walked into the local Woolworth store and sat down at the all-white lunch counter. Before long the sit-ins spread to every state in the Deep South. Enraged laymen spearheaded the new drive for equality. Within a matter of months some seventy thousand Negroes and white people had staged over eight hundred sit-ins in more than one hundred cities. Such mass action served to dramatize Negro demands and compelled the rapid desegregation of many restaurants and other business establishments. Most important, it

[22] *Ibid.*, pp. 123-32. [23] *Ibid.*, pp. 119, 224-35.

vanquished the fear which had previously immobilized most Negroes. "We shall overcome" became the theme song denoting belief in an eventual triumph. The Congress of Racial Equality, twenty years old but little known, was called upon to shape its nonviolent direct action tactics into a formidable art that could be utilized to aid the rebelling students.

Concurrently the sit-ins were augmented by the formation of the Student Non-Violent Coordinating Committee. Though handicapped by a meager budget and staff, SNICK (as it came to be known), under the inspiring leadership of James Forman, stood behind the new protest movement and became a rallying point for Negroes who were dissatisfied with the older civil rights organizations. To supplement and reinforce the sit-ins, another technique, the economic boycott, was devised. In this way adults with purchasing power could stand in the background and sustain the youth who were on the "firing line."[24]

The next step in the Negro revolt came with the freedom rides. On May 4, 1961, six whites and seven Negroes left Washington, D. C., by bus, enroute to New Orleans. When they reached Montgomery a race riot broke out and freedom riders were injured. Federal marshals had to be ordered in and National Guardsmen put on duty. The American Nazi Party made arrangements to send a "hate bus" along the same route. At Jackson, Mississippi, twenty-seven "integrationists" were arrested for seeking service at the white lunch counters and the use of white rest rooms at the bus depot. On final count over a thousand persons were reputed to be involved in the freedom rides. Interstate terminal segregation was almost totally eliminated. When the smoke of battle had cleared it was evident that CORE had emerged as "the boldest and most imaginative organization in the civil rights field."[25] CORE has succeeded in enlisting aggressively-inclined Negroes and whites because it espouses direct action. Its supporters assume credit for desegregating theatres,

[24] *Ibid.*, pp. 133-43. [25] *Ibid.*, p. 156. Cf. pp. 144-55.

employment opportunities and moving toward integrated housing.[26] Some otherwise sympathetic observers have been appalled by what they regard as extremism in the tactics employed by militant-minded CORE members. Blocking motorists on the Triborough Bridge and delaying their arrival at the opening of the World's Fair in 1964, in the judgment of these critics, evoked resentment more than it dramatized grievances. Boorish behavior at the Republican National Convention in San Francisco and the deliberate courting of arrest, it is contended, alienated TV viewers. For Christians who have defended the morality of civil disobedience in the face of injustice there arise the perplexing questions, "How far dare we go?" and "Is there a danger that even the violation of undesirable laws may backfire and help breed a reckless type of lawlessness?"

The most extreme form which the Negro revolt has taken may be seen in the rise of the Honorable Elijah Muhammad, whose disciples are known as the Black Muslims. My initial encounter with this movement came in the fall of 1958 while I was residing in the old Roxbury district of Boston. One afternoon sound trucks blared forth the announcement to our interracial neighborhood that Mr. Muhammad was due to speak the following day at John Hancock Hall on the Muslim challenge to the Negro. Since I was reading the Koran at the time my curiosity was aroused: What was Islam offering the Negro American? Naïvely I decided to attend the publicized meeting and find out. To my amazement the color line was drawn in reverse and I was flatly prohibited from entering the building. No white man allowed!

Only later did I discover that the Black Muslims had mobilized over 100,000 Negroes to preach black supremacy and black union against the white man. In this homegrown Negro religion which bears little actual resemblance to Islam, Elijah Muhammad has convinced his followers that God has decreed the exaltation of the black man. Blacks are under divine approbation. The opposite of

[26] See *This Is CORE,* published by Congress of Racial Equality, 38 Park Row, New York 38, N. Y., n.d.

black is evil, so all white men are evil. The white race is deteriorating and white culture is on the verge of dissolution. The Negro must renounce the way of life established by the white man and scorn peaceful integration. As soon as he separates himself and acquires a new morale, economic self-sufficiency, and high code of ethics, he can anticipate a revival of the pristine glory of his race.[27]

Muhammad Speaks, with the sign of the crescent and the words "the earth belongs to Allah," is published and circulated as the newspaper voice of the black prophet. The headlines reflect the resentment and hatred of a suppressed minority: "A Lawyer's War Against Peonage in the South," "Fight to Free Boston's Slave Maids,"[28] "Muslims Framed to Whitewash the Guilty?" "U. S. Stands Idly By as School Ban Dooms Children."[29]

Negroes with Guns, the provocative book by Robert F. Williams which tells how Negroes molested by the Ku Klux Klan in Monroe, North Carolina, struck back with armed force, was acclaimed by the "Muslims" as an antidote to the "odious . . . perfumed . . . philosophy" of Martin Luther King.[30]

Reputedly some six hundred convicts join the Black Muslims each year. No matter how much one may deplore their racist tenets, one is compelled to admire their work in rehabilitating prisoners and their almost Puritanical renunciation of degrading vices.

In 1963 it appeared that the mantle of the aging "Elijah" would fall on a bellicose "Elisha," the brilliant and self-confident "Malcolm X" who was converted while in a maximum-security prison. Then, early in 1964, disagreements between the two men led to a serious rupture in the movement. Apparently Malcolm's dynamism aroused jealousy among Elijah's family who hoped to inherit the

[27] For a full study of Elijah Muhammad and his movement see C. Eric Lincoln, *The Black Muslims in America* (Boston: Beacon, 1961).

[28] *Muhammad Speaks,* July 19, 1963.

[29] *Ibid.,* August 30, 1963.

[30] Book review by Sylvester Leaks, *Ibid.,* January 31, 1963.

leadership.[31] Waiting for an opportunity to silence the younger man, Muhammad found it after President Kennedy's assassination and Malcolm's comment that it was an instance of "the chickens coming home to roost." Under the veteran leader's explicit order, the fiery upstart was forbidden to make any further public statements, and it seemed that Malcolm's career might be at an end.

After preserving a ninety-day period of silence, however, the irrepressible Malcolm stepped before a TV audience to quip, "It is hard to make a rooster stop crowing once the sun has risen." Excommunicated heretic though he was, his schismatic followers were ready to help him organize his own party. Three elements distinguish this new group of black nationalists: (1) they urge personal independence for the Negro, allowing him to act, speak, and be seen as master of his own home; (2) they propose "self-defense" units—rifle clubs—ready to "execute on the spot" those who threaten Negroes; and (3) they direct their appeal to all Negroes, not just Muslims, allowing cooperation with the interracial civil rights movement. Muhammad is understandably "unhappy" with the break, but insists that it will not deter his own movement which is "divine work."[32]

World Champion Cassius Clay, whose upset victory over Sonny Liston astounded the boxing world, stunned almost everyone with the disclosure that he professes to be a Muslim. Braggadocio Cassius has been eager to offer his opinions to reporters on every conceivable subject including the racial crisis:

> "Forced and token integration is but a temporary and not an everlasting solution to the Negro problem. It is merely a pacifier. . . . I don't want to be blown up. I don't want to be washed down sewers. I just want to be happy with my own kind. . . . I don't join integration marches. I don't pay any attention to all those white women who wink at me. I don't impose myself on people who don't want me."[33]

[31] Cf. *Life* (March 20, 1964).
[32] Cf. G. Samuels, *New York Times Magazine* (March 22, 1964).
[33] "Integration As Negro Champ Sees It," *U. S. News and World Report* (March 16, 1964).

While the crudities of Cassius Clay may be dismissed as the idle mouthings of an eccentric, and the fanaticism of Malcolm X represents only a small portion of the total Negro population, such forms of extremism are potentially explosive. It was long predicted that if white power structures conspired to block Negro advance, the dangerous sparks of black racism could ignite a conflagration that would make previous racial troubles appear like child's play. In places like Harlem and Brooklyn this prediction became a gruesome reality when mobs took to the streets in the summer of 1964. Along with Communist agitators, Black Nationalists were accused of inciting the riots that led to pillaging and bloodshed.

Louis Lomax reports that Muhammad's indictment of Christianity "has deeply shaken the Negro Christian community." Negroes have lost faith in the white man and in the American dream. An ethic which preaches meekness and patience is no longer acceptable. "Through the spellbinding work of Malcolm X . . . the Negro masses [have] become race-conscious in a way they never were before." While most Negroes recognize the fantasy in the beliefs of the new Black Islam, they reject any other "gospel that fails to answer Mohammad's criticism of Christianity."[34] "It is a supreme irony," comments one Christian writer, "that the new black proletariat spawned in the slums of America should now be looking for succor to the fighting faith that mortally challenged Christianity in eastern Europe centuries ago."[35]

The Black Muslims deliberately reject the fundamental premises and values implicit in the American creed. They are "outsiders" who want a separate domain of their own. The United States Constitution, Muhammad says, was only intended for white citizens. It is futile for Negroes to seek liberation under its provisions. An open and permanent rupture between black and white is inevitable in his expectation.

[34] Lomax, *op. cit.*, pp. 187-92.

[35] Arthur B. Southwick, "Malcolm X: Charismatic Demagogue," *Christian Century* (June 5, 1963), p. 741.

Most Americans, Negro and Caucasian, disagree. For them the Declaration of Independence is a cherished ideal. The phrase affirming that "all men are created equal" may not apply to native intellectual endowment, but it should, in their estimation, be actualized in according everyone as much equality of opportunity as possible. The Bill of Rights should guarantee to all respect for their personal liberties. The "irrepressible conflict" divided the North and the South because the cancer of slavery had been permitted to fester and threaten the health of the Union. The Emancipation Proclamation, according to this interpretation, was a moral victory over that abominable evil which permitted human beings to be held in bondage. When Lincoln spoke on January 1, 1863, his was the voice of a revived American conscience. The righteousness of the country was vindicated.

Obviously this is an over-simplification. Slavery was not the only evil that gnawed away at the vitals of the nation's moral and spiritual strength. Not every slaveholder was inhumane. Northern abolitionists could rightfully be reprimanded for failing to see "the log in their own eyes" while they were self-righteously extracting the "specks" from their neighbors to the south.

Yet it remains undeniable that slavery and its aftermath of Jim Crowism, lynchings, and Negro suppression are among the worst stains on American honor; and even today they remain the unlifted burden on the Christian conscience. Moral fervor reached a peak during the crusade against "that peculiar institution" which, not discounting the Social Gospel era, has not been duplicated until our own day. Now, once again in the struggle against segregation, the idealists in a younger generation have found a moral cause with which they can identify themselves. Church conventions have passed resolutions denouncing all forms of racial discrimination, and at least some clergymen have taken heroic action in advocating open housing or joining freedom rides. More than a few of these twentieth-century abolitionists have lost their pulpits or languished in prison cells. Rededication to the goal of emancipation has gone far toward awakening the dormant Christian conscience.[36]

[36] Cf. Editorial, "Regrouped, Renewed, Reforming," *Christian Century* (December 4, 1963), p. 1489: "Confronted by the nonviolent civil rights revolution, the ecumenical churches and their National Council have cast their weight on the side of the oppressed. . . . They have crossed their spiritual Rubicon and are heavily engaged on a thousand fronts. Today denominational leaders and pastors as well as laymen, whites as well as Negroes, students as well as grandfathers, know the smell of prison life against the inside, the feel of police brutality, the frustration of judicial contempt. Many have been ostracized and harassed; some have lost their jobs; some have lost their lives, and the struggle has indeed only begun."

2 Church and Slavery from Ancient Times to the Settlement of the New World

Sometimes the claim is made that the Christian church took the lead in extirpating the slavery system. Holding the opposite view, Ernst Troeltsch was convinced that the teachings and practice of the church constituted one of the main sanctions for its perpetuation.[1] The truth perhaps lies somewhere in between.

Slavery existed throughout the history of antiquity and was usually regarded as an inevitable condition. To justify the Greek ambition for universal hegemony, Aristotle evolved the hypothesis that certain peoples are worthy of being free from birth, while others are naturally intended for slavery. It would be inaccurate and unfair to pretend that this position was uncontested in the pagan world before the advent of Christianity. During the Hellenistic peroid the dissolution of the Greek city-states and the expansion of commerce contributed to a more cosmopolitan outlook that disavowed concepts of inequality. Although not always consistent in his break from the Aristotelian belief, Cicero once wrote: "Men differ in knowledge but all are equal in ability to learn; there is no race which, guided by reason, cannot obtain virtue."[2] The Stoic

[1] See Ernst Troeltsch, *The Social Teachings of the Christian Church* (New York: Harper, 1960), I, 133.

[2] Juan Comas, *Racial Myths* (Paris: UNESCO, 1951), p. 6.

philosophers were more emphatic in their repudiation of "natural" aristocracies of wealth and privilege. Men like Seneca and Epictetus argued that there were no slaves in the primitive state. Only beasts were irrational creatures. Since slaves were human they should be treated with consideration and kindness.

Under the influence of such enlightened philosophies the Roman emperors at times eased the lot of the slaves. Claudius issued an imperial command in A.D. 41 that sick slaves who had been abandoned by their masters should be freed. Vespasian ordered the liberation of slave women whose masters prostituted them. Domitian in 81 prohibited, under the penalty of death, the mutilation of slaves. It must be admitted that until the collapse of the Roman Empire the church continued to sanction slavery, and did not seem to advance much beyond the views expressed by its pagan contemporaries. The Church Fathers usually acquiesced in the injustices of the prevailing social order and helped to preserve it by counseling obedience on the part of slaves toward their owners.

Irenaeus, Bishop of Lyons in the latter half of the second century, made a distinction between two types of offering, the "servile" and the "pure" sacrifice. The offering of a sincere and righteous slave might be a sweet savor in the nostrils of God, but not nearly so sweet as that of a free man! Chrysostom, the famous bishop and preacher of Constantinople, ascribed the origin of slavery to sin.[3] The persistence of slavery was explained all too conveniently by reference to the fall of man. "Slavery," said Augustine, "has been imposed by the just sentence of God upon the sinner." It is God's prescribed remedy for the moral degredation into which some men have fallen.[4] St. Isadore spoke of the inner freedom of mind which the slave may have in spite of bondage and adds:

> Better is humble servitude than proud liberty. . . . In consequence of

[3] William L. Westermann, *The Slave Systems of Greek and Roman Antiquity* (Philadelphia: American Philosophical Society, 1955), p. 157.

[4] Rayford W. Logan, "The Attitude of the Church Toward Slavery Prior to 1500," *The Journal of Negro History,* XVII, 469.

the sin of the first man, the penalty of slavery was brought by God on the human race, so that they whom He saw less fit for liberty, might more mercifully be punished with slavery.[5]

As the medieval church grew in wealth and power it accepted slave labor for use in its own institutions. Thus, at the beginning of the eighth century the Abbey of St. Germain-des-Prés had eight thousand slaves, St. Martin of Tours had twenty thousand, the church at Villiers several thousand. The kings of France were encouraged to give slaves to the church. The Venetians sold Christian slaves to the Saracens, and with part of the profit built shrines for the saints.[6] It is alleged that at the beginning of the Crusades ninety-five percent of the population of Europe were either in slavery or serfdom. There is little evidence that the hierarchy of the church showed any pity or concern for their plight.

Nevertheless, the church did lend its moral support to the provisions of the Roman law which restrained the arbitrary power of the master, protected the slaves, and added its own penalties to the enforcement of these laws. There is little doubt that the conditions under which slaves lived were improved where the Christian love ethic permeated the lives of people. Masters were admonished to be kind to their slaves. Slave and free attended the same church and communed at the same table. Slaves could rise to the priesthood. Pope Callixtus is said to have been a fugitive slave. Christian tombstones did not proclaim the social status of the deceased. The church did not approve of the forcible separation of husbands and wives who were slaves. Some writers declared emancipation to be a meritorious act.[7] Slaves were to be exempted from work on Sunday. What the church insisted upon in contradistinction from

[5] *Ibid.*, p. 478.

[6] Will Durant, *The Age of Faith* (New York: Simon and Schuster, 1950), p. 454.

[7] One of the strongest pleas was voiced by Gregory the Great: "Since our Redeemer, the Author of all life, deigned to take human flesh, that by the power of His Godhead, the chains by which we were held in bondage being broken, He might restore us to our first state of liberty, it is most fitting that men by

the non-Christian world was upholding the true humanity and the sacredness of the personality of the slave because his soul was created by God.

The Reformation era did not bring any forthright denunciation of slavery except on the part of some of the radical reformers like Thomas Muentzer, who was discredited because of his apocalypticism and extreme belligerency. Luther and Calvin were preoccupied with theological issues and were cautious and conservative in their approach to the social order. At first sympathetic toward the grievances of the oppressed peasantry, Luther was alarmed when they resorted to violence, and turned against them. His attitude toward slavery is partially depicted in his rejoinder to the Third Article of the Peasants: "There shall be no serfs, for Christ has made all men free." Luther replied:

> That is making Christian liberty an utterly carnal thing. Did not Abraham and other patriarchs and prophets have slaves? Read what St. Paul teaches about servants, who, at that time were all slaves. Therefore this article is dead against the Gospel. It is a piece of robbery by which every man takes from his lord the body, which has become his lord's property. For a slave can be a Christian, and have Christian liberty, in the same way that a prisoner or a sick man is a Christian, and yet not free. This article would make all men equal, and turn the spiritual kingdom of Christ into a worldly, external kingdom; and that is impossible. For a worldly kingdom cannot stand unless there is in it an inequality of persons, so that some are free, some imprisoned, some lords, some subjects.[8]

As might be expected, the men of the Enlightenment were generally against slavery as in conflict with their cherished theories

the concession of manumission should restore to the freedom in which they were born those whom nature sent free into the world, but who have been condemned to the yoke of slavery by the Law of Nations." Quoted by Logan, *op. cit.*, p. 473. Used by permission of the publisher, The Association for the Study of Negro Life and History, Inc.

[8] In *Admonition to Peace* (Works of Martin Luther, Vol. IV [6 vols.; Philadelpiha: A. J. Holman Co., 1915-1932]), p. 240.

about the natural rights of man. But there were differences of opinion as to the equality of races. Montaigne said:

> There is nothing savage or barbarous about [the Brazilian Indian] save for the fact that each of us labels whatever is not among his own customs of his own peoples as barbarism.[9]

Voltaire and Rousseau believed in the equality of all men regardless of racial origin. David Hume, on the contrary, was inclined to believe that Negroes were naturally inferior to whites.[10] The church lagged behind the philosophers and said little to rebuke the profiteers who trafficked in human bodies.

Slavery had flourished among the Assyrians, the Persians, the Egyptians, and the Carthaginians. The Greeks enslaved those whom they conquered, and (as already noted) their philosophers approved. The intellectuals of the ancient world argued that some people had slave minds, and if left to themselves, were unhappy.

Slavery did not originally imply the subjugation of Negroes by whites. Extreme color consciousness is largely a modern phenomenon in which slaves and degradation came to be associated almost exclusively with a dark skin. The slaves in Babylon or Rome could be different in complexion, depending upon what racial stock had been defeated and led into captivity. For centuries when the Muslims of North Africa waged war against European countries many thousands of white men were captured and held as slaves.

Nor were whites the only culprits in the accumulation of slaves. Black Muslims inciting racial hatred in our country today have fabricated a myth in depicting Africa as an idyllic land of freedom and tranquility before the arrival of the white man. Actually, slavery was practiced in Africa long before the interference of Europeans. Among the pastoral tribes of the West Coast misconduct or debt could reduce the accused to slave status. A man who violated the prevailing code by stealing or killing could be sold into

[9] Comas, *op. cit.*, pp. 7, 8. [10] *Ibid.*

slavery instead of being executed. Not uncommonly, enslavement was the dire consequence of being captured in war. The lust for power and the capacity for moral evil is by no means restricted to one race.

Nevertheless, the fact remains that the greed and ambition of "Christian" traders and colonists caused some of the most flagrant evils that have ever been recorded.

When the enslavement of Africans became financially advantageous for the growing commercial class in Europe, moral scruples suddenly vanished. The "Christians" of Portugal took the lead and organized expeditions for the capture of slaves in 1441. Soon "a slave market was set up in Lisbon, and in the second half of the fifteenth century there were regular yearly shipments of human cargoes from Angola and Mozambique. It is reckoned that in 1537 as many as 10,000 slaves were shipped across the Atlantic."[11]

The merchants of Spain and England did not wish to be excluded from the accruing profits and ordered their ships in the direction of the "dark continent." The daring buccaneer, John Hawkins, was knighted by Queen Elizabeth for his prowess in acquiring human merchandise and was given command of a squadron of seven ships to transport slaves from Africa to the West Indies. As the British Empire expanded overseas, the clamor for more slaves became louder. From Cape Verde to the Equator military forts were built for defense against rival traders and as detention centers where slaves were kept until they could be transported to America. During the seventeenth and eighteenth centuries the Dutch, the Germans, and the Danes joined in the grim business and constructed their own fortifications.

Slaves were acquired by African chiefs when they defeated neighboring tribes and took prisoners, or when they held debtors to work out their debts, or when they imposed a penalty upon men who desecrated or removed someone else's fetish. Thus war, crime, and

[11] H. Russell, *Human Cargoes* (London: Longmans, Green and Co., 1948), p. 20.

superstition provided a supply of servants who were available for sale to white men. To propitiate the chiefs, entertainment, presents, and drink were provided aboard the vessels of the traders. Unrestrained debauchery was encouraged. Deceit and treachery of all kinds were then employed to persuade the African rulers to seize strong, well-built men who would bring a high price on the market. Kidnapping was common. Chiefs who had a grudge against a native tribe were incited to take revenge by capturing and selling the offenders. Supposedly civilized captains from Christian lands engaged in what is known as the badger game, whereby attractive wives were induced to ensnare unsuspecting amorous swains. "They made money out of it, and the ship merchants and stockholders in the ships knew that it was done and willingly shared the profits."[12]

As the demand for slaves increased, every scruple of conscience seems to have been discarded. At its beginning the trade had been an exchange of a certain amount of goods for individuals legally held as slaves. Eventually a majority of every cargo purchased consisted of free men drawn into captivity through trickery or compulsion. The next step was to resort to piracy—planned attacks on natives who refused to trade. Soon thereafter came the practice of goading the coastal tribes into making raids on the interior. Defeated Negroes who were not killed in these forays were carried down to the sea and sold. As the greed for "black ivory" mounted even higher the white slavers did not shrink away from direct participation in the bloody deeds.

The plight of African slaves was extremely pitiful. Mothers were torn from their children and husbands were separated from their wives. Only physically sturdy men and women who were equipped to withstand the arduous labor of the American plantations were retained. The elderly, the sick, and the weaklings were likely to be slaughtered without mercy. During the weary journey from the interior to the coast the heavily loaded captives were com-

[12] John R. Spears, *The American Slave Trade* (New York: Ballantine Books, 1960), p. 42.

pelled to march from dawn to dusk in blazing heat and in torrents of rain through dense jungles and across rivers infested by crocodiles. If they faltered and collapsed from exhaustion they were severely beaten. If they failed to rise they were finished off by the stroke of a sword or the blow of a club. Sometimes, if they were incapacitated, they were abandoned in the bush where they endured the pangs of hunger, thirst, and disease until relieved by death.[13]

No wonder that ship captains and slave holders preferred to think of the Negro as sub-human or sheer animal! The cruelties imposed might otherwise disturb even the most insensitive profiteer. In his short history of the African slave trade Henry Russell provides this gruesome description:

> The survivors who reached the coast were driven naked into the market like cattle. Burning irons, with the name of the company or buyer were then applied—often on the naked breast—in spite of the groans of the strong men and the screams of the women. . . . Then came the horrors of the sea voyage. Tied in groups of six, necks and ankles chained together, these hopeless sufferers were pushed into the hold, without clothing or beds, where neither light nor fresh air could reach them. They were forced to sleep on wooden shelves. . . . Each slave was fastened to a ring-bolt in the floor or to an iron bar running the whole length of the shelf. . . . In some cases the ships were so tightly packed with their human cargo that the unfortunate passengers had only eighteen inches between the shelves—hardly as much space as a man in his coffin!
>
> Maize and water once every twenty-four hours was their only food. If the slaves refused to eat they were lashed and if they failed, hot irons were used to force them to eat. . . . The frightful stench, the poor food, the stifling heat and the cruel treatment soon began to show their ill effects. . . . During the voyage the average death rate was between seven and eight per cent, a large number dying of suffocation.[14]

To avoid paying the duty which was assessed on slaves that died

[13] See Russell, *op. cit.,* p. 27. [14] *Ibid.,* pp. 28-29.

soon after landing it became advantageous to exterminate the sick. If the water supply was running short it was not uncommon to cast some of the human cargo into the sea. (In 1781 on the British slaver *Tong* 132 slaves were dropped overboard to save enough water for the remainder.) To the avaricious mind the reasoning behind such decisions was simple enough. If the slaves died a natural death—due to thirst—the loss would fall upon the owners, but if they were drowned the loss was covered by insurance.

There are abundant eye witness accounts to verify the evils involved in the barter for human bodies. As late as November 30, 1845, the Yorktown Commander Bell captured the American bark *Pons* with 896 slaves on board. Anyone not hardened to human anguish will shudder at his testimony:

> The vessel has no slave-deck, and upwards of one hundred and fifty were piled, almost in bulk, on water-casks below. As the ship appeared to be less than three hundred and fifty tons, it seemed impossible that one-half could have lived to cross the Atlantic. About two hundred filled up the spar-deck alone when they were permitted to come up from below; and yet the captain assured me that it was his intention to have taken four hundred more on board if he could have spared the time.
>
> The stench from below was so great that it was impossible to stand more than a few minutes near the hatchways. Our men who went below from curiosity, were forced up sick in a few minutes: then all the hatches were off. What must have been the sufferings of those poor wretches when the hatches were closed! I am informed that very often in these cases, the stronger will strangle the weaker; and this was probably the reason why so many died, or rather were found dead the morning after the capture. None but an eye-witness can form a conception of the horrors these poor creatures must endure in their transit across the ocean.[15]

A ship's surgeon, named Falconbridge, gave the following evidence before an official court of inquiry:

[15] W. O. Blake, *The History of Slavery and the Slave Trade* (Columbus, Ohio: J. and H. Miller, 1857), p. 306.

> The men Negroes on being brought aboard are immediately fastened two by two by handcuffs on their wrists and by irons riveted on their legs. They are frequently stowed so close as to admit of no other posture than lying on their sides. . . . When the Negroes refused to take sustenance, I have seen coals of fire, glowing hot, put on a shovel and placed so near their lips as to scorch and burn them. . . . The deck, which is the floor of their rooms, was so covered with blood and mucous from their excreta that it resembled a slaughterhouse.[16]

When confronted by these atrocities of "the middle passage" the Christian conscience recoils. Quite likely the average church member will agree that these crimes were "an abomination unto the Lord." "But what do these past transgressions against God and man have to do with me now?" he objects. "I cannot be held responsible for the inhumanities and abuses of past generations! I would never condone or participate in such brutalities."

But the fact is that we cannot escape our continuity with the past. We are embroiled in the troublous consequences of centuries of slavery. Political controversies in our country and the social tensions which perturb us are derived, in large measure, from this heritage of evil. Whether they admit it or not, diehard segregationists, North or South, have preserved the mentality of unreconstructed slaveholders. And we have all been infected by the poisonous ideas and practices spread by the proponents of slavery and their "white supremacy" successors. Pathetically enough all of us are inextricably enmeshed in one way or another in the diabolical snare of racism. No one can detach himself completely from the sins of his forefathers and protest his absolute innocence. What have we done to remove the stigma of slavery from the Negro? Have we not shared in economic aggrandizement or class privileges based on the exploitation of ex-slaves? How many of us can deny that we have subscribed to or given silent assent to the myth of assumed Negro inferiority?

The sensitized Christian conscience can still hear the moans of

[16] Russell, *op. cit.,* pp. 30-32.

suffering slaves and plead for mercy and forgiveness based on the deeds of the crucified Servant of God. At the same time a historical survey of the church's involvement in slavery should induce in us more than pangs of regret and a righting of our broken relationship with God. It should move us to work toward the goal of full emancipation for all of God's children on earth.

3 Slavery in America

The Spaniards who settled in the New World were unwilling to engage in the arduous toil that was necessary to cultivate their rich plantations and extract gold and silver from the mines in Mexico and Peru. The severity of the climate, no doubt, contributed to their aversion to manual labor. After the conquests of Pizzaro and Cortez, many American Indians were enslaved and compelled to work in the fields and the mines. Maltreated, and physically unable to endure the strain, they came to be regarded as unfit for forced labor.

Las Casas, a missionary in the West Indies, was moved by compassion for the wretched natives to propose that Africans be imported as substitutes. According to his eyewitness report he relates:

> I once beheld four or five Indian chiefs roasted on a slow fire. Their screams disturbed the sleep of the commanding officer, so he gave orders that they should be strangled. The officer on guard . . . would not allow this. He caused their mouths to be gagged that their cries might not be heard, stirred up the fire with his own hands, and roasted them until they expired.[1]

When Columbus discovered Haiti it had an estimated population of over one million. Forty years later this number was decimated

[1] H. Russell, *Human Cargoes* (London: Longmans, Green and Co., 1948), p. 13.

to five hundred. The Spanish colonial empire in America was threatened with collapse. The acquisition of Negroes from across the ocean to replace the expiring Indians was the plan adopted. The climates of Haiti and West Africa seemed much alike, and it was assumed that the Negroes would have sufficient stamina to survive both the heat and the toil.

As for the North American mainland, forms of voluntary and involuntary servitude accompanied colonization. When a Dutch ship entered the James River in 1619 with twenty African slaves who were purchased by the colonists at Jamestown, Virginia, it marked the beginning of slavery in the American colonies. As long as there was a considerable supply of indentured servants from England, the use of Negroes was rather limited. During the early colonial period the Africans generally shared the same status as white servants. Their treatment was relatively humane, and it was not unusual for them to attain their freedom.

Toward the end of the seventeenth century, however, the supply of indentured servants diminished, and the demand for Negro slaves increased. After the Treaty of Utrecht, England assumed a dominant role in the slave trade. Between the years 1713 and 1733, fifteen thousand slaves were imported annually in ships carrying the British flag, with over half of them destined for the colonies along the Atlantic seaboard. Almost immediately the New England towns of Boston and Newport became deeply implicated in the infamous three-cornered slave traffic. (Molasses from the West Indies was brought to New England, made into rum, and taken back to Africa in exchange for more slaves which were sold to the West Indies and the colonies.) By 1801 the total population of slaves in the United States stood at 1,007,037.[2]

The great bulk of the slaves was centered in the South because

[2] See Leonard L. Haynes, Jr., *The Negro Community within American Protestantism, 1619-1844* (Boston: Christopher, 1953), pp. 13-34. The undeniable involvement of New Englanders in this profiteering made it difficult for them to assume a "better than thou" attitude toward the South in the slavery controversy.

the institution of compulsory bondage was not so financially advantageous in the North. When slaves were kept in New England, for the most part, they were not physically abused. Negroes in New England were usually used as domestic servants and were not infrequently admitted to the family circle and encouraged to receive religious instruction. In the southern colonies slaves were found useful primarily as plantation laborers. Many of them were kept on a subsistence level and were constantly under the threat of his master's lash.

The growing Negro community presented an embarrassing dilemma to a young nation struggling against British tyranny and clamoring for political freedom. It seemed like a grotesque absurdity for slave owners to sign a Declaration of Independence which affirmed the inalienable right of every man to liberty and equality. Few, if any, of the founding fathers, were prepared to endorse full equality for the Negro. They were benevolent aristocrats rather than equalitarian democrats. Yet, through their writings and public utterances, men like Jefferson, Franklin, and Paine indicated that they were aware of the inconsistency of espousing freedom and practicing slavery, and they were disturbed by it.

During the colonial and revolutionary period of American history, Protestants developed the idea that the Negro community should be permitted to share in the moral benefits of Christianity. The denominations of this period defended equality in religion regardless of a man's social status or racial origin. Quite commonly the Negro was granted the right to worship with the white congregation and participate in church life. Where assemblies for worship were composed exclusively of Negroes it was taken for granted that they would be welcome to share in the wider fellowship and associational life of the church body. There are even records of Negro preachers who served as pastors of white congregations. A few churches prompted by their leaders took action against slavery. Dr. Samuel Hopkins aroused his slaveholding and trading congregation in Newport, Rhode Island, to oppose slavery about 1769. The Quaker, John Woolman, an eyewitness to the cruelties perpetrated by slaveholders in the middle of the eighteenth century, took an outspoken stand against slavery and testified against it at every opportunity:

> These are a people who have made no agreement to serve us, and who have not forfeited their liberty that we know of. These are the souls for whom Christ died, and for our conduct towards them we must answer before that Almighty Being who is no respector of persons.[3]

The period from 1800 to 1831 may best be characterized as transitional and conducive to a gradual change in attitude among clergymen both North and South. While there was no aggressive concerted action demanding the immediate emancipation of the Negro, theological discussion and economic change were preparing the way for the anti-slavery trumpet blasts that were to come. The sentiments directed against the slavery system at this time were like smouldering embers waiting for certain historical incidents and qualified leadership to fan the embers into bright flames. It was a time of preparation during which the rift between North and South was deepening. The invention of Eli Whitney's cotton gin revolutionized economic life in the slave states. An enormous vested interest demanded the protection and expansion of an economy dependent upon enforced servitude. The lines were being drawn and the stage was being set for the bitter sectional strife which would lead to "the irrepressible conflict." Men like Whittier and Emerson were mildly pleading the cause of the Negro through the medium of poetry, but the New England mind was unruffled until William Lloyd Garrison launched *The Liberator* and his verbal onslaughts began to charge the atmosphere. Most of the

[3] Harry Emerson Fosdick, "The Journal of John Woolman," *Great Voices of the Reformation* (New York: Random House, 1952), p. 485.

denominations were willing to preserve a discreet silence in order to placate pro-slavery elements in their membership. In such cases, the cause of slavery gained strength.

The tendency toward segregation in the churches was gaining favor. A caste consciousness was taking shape in the organizational structure of the Protestant churches. Rather than suffer from discrimination, the Negroes withdrew to start independent church movements. In the South, Negro preachers spearheaded slave revolts in protest against the increased severity of their burden. Inspired by biblically derived apocalyptic visions, they sought to establish the "New Jerusalem" by force. In the North, Negroes formed societies and wrote pamphlets dedicated to the cause of freedom for their racial kinsmen.[4]

Most of the Calvinistic-orientated theocrats of the North assumed that the Negro could not be assimilated in a "white" society. Many were induced to endorse the American Colonization Society which proposed the establishment of a Negro Republic in Liberia to be populated with transplanted slaves from the United States. Some envisioned the new colony as a base of operations for the future evangelization of Africa. Others looked upon colonization as an excellent safety valve against the danger to national security which a quarter million colored freedmen seemed to represent.[5]

After 1831, the accusations of the abolitionists, the controversy over the admission of Missouri as a state, and several slave rebellions combined to solidify the South in its defense of slavery. Under these provocations southern spokesmen abandoned their former apologetic attitude and announced themselves as unashamed champions of a social system which they found desirable and practical. In political life the moderate leadership of Virginia yielded to the recalcitrants from South Carolina. Slavery was not only an

[4] Cf. Haynes, *op. cit.*, pp. 79-121, 213-18.

[5] Cf. John R. Bodo, *The Protestant Clergy and Public Issues, 1812-1848* (Princeton: Princeton University Press, 1954), pp. 112-32.

economic necessity for the stabilization of an ideal Athenian-like society, but it was a "positive good" which provided for the benevolent protection of the weaklings and inferiors who would otherwise be unable to survive. The theory of reciprocal obligations, based on precedents in feudalism, and nourished by the romantic novels of Sir Walter Scott, argued that slavery was the best foundation for an enduring economic order in which the subservience of the lower class was rewarded by the paternal generosity of the upper class. A favorite retort of southerners who were piqued by northern self-righteousness was to point to the impoverishment and miserable working conditions endured by "free" workers in New England factory towns. Was slavery really so reprehensible when it at least guaranteed enough provisions for physical sustenance and eliminated the haunting fear of unemployment? In a northerner like Orestes Brownson[6] they found an ally who agreed that slavery was preferable to the evils of the factory system.

In the latter half of the eighteenth century, humanitarians in England began to crusade in favor of abolishing the slave trade. Granville Sharp and Thomas Clarkson, prominent members of the Society for the Abolition of the Slave Trade (founded in 1787), argued that enforced servitude was incompatible with the English legal concepts of liberty. Leader of the fight in Parliament was the renowned William Wilberforce whose oratorical eloquence was effectively enlisted in the battle against the gruesome traffic in human bodies until the slave trade was terminated in 1807.

In the United States the first national act to curb the slave trade became law in 1794, but states remained free to make their own decisions about the legality of bringing in more slaves from Africa. When the acquisition of more Negro laborers for the cotton fields

[6] The erratic philosopher-pamphleteer whose passionate quest for truth led him from Universalism to New England transcendentalism to socialist thought to the Roman Catholic church. Politically he became a supporter of John Calhoun. In minority rights he saw the one safeguard against the rule of consolidated capital. He advised abolitionists to display their philanthropy in the poverty-stricken slums of the north. See Arthur M. Schlesinger, Jr., *Orestes A. Brownson, A Pilgrim's Progress* (Boston: Little, Brown and Co., 1939).

seemed crucial for economic gain, South Carolina repealed her law forbidding slave imports. Among other southern states smuggling became a lucrative racket. Illicit operations multiplied where prohibitory measures were introduced. So bold and frequent did the violations become that the decade before the Civil War saw an actual increase in the "infernal traffic."[7]

The Christian conscience in the South remained dormant. Most churchmen preferred to "look the other way" and never see their colored brethren who had "fallen among the thieves." Those sensitive souls who were squeamish about the blood drawn by the lash and the agony of mothers separated from their children, and may have been inclined to protest, were cowed into silence by the preponderance of pro-slavery opinion. Some of the stalwart southern opponents of slavery gradually withdrew and resettled in the North.

The abolitionists contended that little had been done to help Negroes in this country spiritually or materially. Many clergymen conceded the failure of the churches in this regard and were disturbed by the malignant evil which continued to fester in the land. Some continued to hope for a solution through a gradual and voluntary resettlement in Africa. Some southern churchmen conscientiously endeavored to instruct and evangelize the colored people in their midst, but often their efforts were blocked by obdurate slaveholders who feared that literacy and the inculcation of Christian ideals would interfere with unrestricted exploitation of the Negro slaves.[8]

Exposés of slavery are loaded with abundant data to demonstrate how savage and heartless men (and women) can become when they are given unlimited power over other human beings. A visitor to Charleston, South Carolina, tells how he passed along one of the main streets one day and heard a loud roar of laughter mingled

[7] Cf. W. E. B. DuBois, *The Suppression of the African Slave-Trade to the United States of America, 1638-1870* (New York: Social Science Press, 1954), pp. 178-87.

[8] Cf. *Ibid.*, pp. 132-51.

with exclamations of derision erupting from a gathering crowd. When he arrived on the scene he recalls:

> I saw a poor broken-hearted, half-distracted woman, the mother of a child whom these devils of the block had torn from her bosom and sold to strangers, never more perhaps to be seen by that mother in this life. She wept and raved, and tore like a maniac. . . . The babe was borne in one direction and the mother in another. Her fruitless, heart-broken efforts, and screams of distress at the result, made mirth for the heartless unfeeling multitude. They laughed, hooted and mocked at her misfortune, as though they were dumb beasts that were thus separated.[9]

Theodore Weld, a convert of the Finney revivals and one of the founders of Lane Seminary, detailed the viciousness of the slavery system. In 1839 he published *American Slavery As It Is,* the "testimony of a thousand witnesses," which became the standard reference work for the abolitionists. The personal narratives of ministers who had lived in the South were incorporated along with advertisements from southern newspapers calling for the return of runaway slaves who could be recognized by the scars inflicted by frequent floggings. The privations of the slaves were described in terms of meager diet,[10] inadequate clothing, unsanitary living conditions, wretched housing, overwork in the fields, and neglect of the sick. None of the gory details was spared. The daughter of a South Carolina judge revealed how the fashionabily elite of Charleston saw no contradiction between their affiliation with a Christian church and their unmerciful whipping of slaves. She relates that the same woman who opened her house to prayer meetings and moved about in the best aristocratic circles so lacerated the backs of her slaves that their flesh became putrid. She tells

[9] Philo Tower in *Slavery Unmasked.* Quoted by Richard Roscoe Miller, *Slavery and Catholicism* (Durham, N. C.: North State Publishers, 1957), p. 145.

[10] In North Carolina the legal allowance of food for slaves was a "quart of corn per day." In most slave states it was left to the option of the masters.

about a gentleman renowned for his benevolence who injured the eye of a ten-year-old boy by the blow of a cowhide so severely that the sight was destroyed.[11] She mentioned mangling, imprisonment, and starvation as tortures which were commonly meted out to slaves as punishments for indolence or disobedience. Almost half of the book is devoted to objections to the incredible cruelties and to the assumption that the self-interest of the masters and public opinion could be relied upon to serve as deterrents to unrestrained abuse. The cumulative effect of this catalogue of horrors is staggering and can only leave the most inhumane unmoved by sympathy. Even if it be granted that Weld's presentation of slavery is exaggerated and one-sided, the documented facts speak for themselves and are irrefutable evidence that the system was indefensible from a Christian standpoint.

American literature during the 1830's and 1840's was surprisingly silent on the slavery debate which was rocking the Union. For the most part, the transcendentalists of New England were preoccupied with other concerns. There were a few exceptions, however. Whittier published a number of anti-slavery poems, and Longfellow came through a little later (1842) with his *Poems on Slavery.* Bronson Alcott and Henry Thoreau took exception to the Mexican War as a conflict undertaken to appease the slavocracy's lust for land, as Lowell had done in the first series of *The Bigelow Papers* (1846). Otherwise, the overwhelming majority of poets and essayists appeared to be oblivious to the most serious moral problem in the nation's history.

Sentimental novelists were inclined to pass over the sordid realities of slavery, and chose to provide excitment through exotic characterizations that would have to be dismissed as escapist fantasies. Nonetheless it was a product of the sentimentalist tradition that swept over North and South like a cyclone and did more to create sympathy for the slaves than the sum total of all the abolitionist

[11] Testimony of Angelina Grunke Weld in *American Slavery As It Is* (New York: American Anti-Slavery Society, 1839), pp. 52-57.

writings. *Uncle Tom's Cabin* was the supreme tear-jerker and has been discredited for a presumed lack of art. Yet it did not call upon its readers to evade the gruesome facts but rather to confront them, to be moved to pity, and then to act to eradicate this blight on society. Throughout the novel the horror of slavery is pressed upon the reader in scenes of domestic anarchy (e.g., the suicide by drowning of the slave woman whose child has just been sold and taken from her forever) and moral degradation (as portrayed in the loathsome figure of Simon Legree).[12]

Harriet Beecher Stowe's "best seller" has been ridiculed for perpetuating some of the comic stereotypes that found their way into minstrel shows. "Uncle Tom" has become a synonym for meek subservience—a characterization thoroughly repudiated by the militant Negroes of the present generation. A closer look, however, shows that the book remains a devastating indictment of slavery. The field hands who are shiftless, the house servants who are dishonest, the black overseers who are brutally tyrannical, and the mulatto wenches who are debauched by drink and sex are all the deplorable and vicious outcome of an ungodly system. If the Negro has been debased, and if he is filled with vices, the fault lies primarily with the white man who has robbed him of his basic humanity and deprived him of all the incentives for advancement and achievement which motivate and sustain his own race. Topsy seems to lack any sense of moral values and is insensitive to punishment because she never knew the loving care of a mother or father and has become inured to hardships. Prue has degenerated into a disgusting, depraved, "old, cut-up critter" who drowns her woes in alcohol because she was long treated like an animal to breed slaves for the market and is tormented by her bitter memories. Where do these horrid outrages come from, St. Clare asks himself in conversation with his cousin Ophelia, and answers:

[12] See Kenneth S. Lynn in his introduction to Harriet Beecher Stowe, *Uncle Tom's Cabin* (Cambridge, Mass.: Harvard University Press, 1962), pp. vii, x, xi.

> "In many cases, it is a gradual hardening process on both sides,—the owner growing more and more cruel, as the servant more and more callous. Whipping and abuse are like laudanum; you have to double the dose as the sensibilities decline."[13]

Southern aristocrats and northern romanticists alike conjured up an image of happy plantation life with the carefree, childlike Negro laughing and singing and looking up to his benevolent "white father" as friend and benefactor. Mrs. Stowe demolishes this "myth" through the scornful comment of St. Clare:

> "It's all nonsense to talk to me about slaves *enjoying* all this! . . . I have no patience with the unutterable trash that some of your patronizing Northerners have made up, as in their zeal to apologize for our sins. We all know better."[14]

Uneasy Christian consciences in the South excused the severities of their system by pointing an accusing finger at the northerners and the British who exploited helpless laborers. St. Clare agrees that slavery is not the only injustice being inflicted in the world, but finds no consolation in the thought:

> . . . the American planter is "only doing in another form what the English aristocracy and capitalists are doing by the lower classes"; that is . . . *appropriating* [italics in the original] them, body and bone, soul and spirit, to their use and convenience. . . . The English laborer is as much at the will of his employer as if he were sold to him. The slave-owner can whip his refractory slave to death,—the capitalist can starve him to death. . . . But it's no kind of apology for slavery.[15]

[13] Stowe, *op. cit.*, p. 252.
[14] *Ibid.*, p. 234.
[15] *Ibid.*, p. 235.

4 The Theological Defense of Slavery

There were four major events in the four decades between 1780 and 1820 that had important implications for the slave population in the United States. The first was the Ordinance for the Northwest Territory in 1787 which covered all land north of the Ohio River and westward to the Mississippi, ceded by Great Britain. Unambiguously expressing the growing conviction of the states lying north of the Mason-Dixon line it affirmed: "There shall be neither slavery nor involuntary servitude otherwise than in the punishment of crimes whereof the party shall have been duly convicted." By this date all of the New England states had abolished slavery altogether and Pennsylvania had provided for gradual emancipation.

The second major event was the framing of the federal constitution, adopted in 1788, which recognized the existence of slavery in veiled language, to effect a compromise between divergent views and bickering states, and gave tacit assent to its legitimacy.[1]

Implementing section two of Article IV of the Constitution was the first Fugitive Slave Act of 1793. By this law the federal government assumed responsibility for the return of runaway slaves.

[1] In the Constitution the word "slave" is not mentioned, yet slaves do not count as full people. Article I, Section 2 states that representatives and taxes shall be apportioned according to the number of free persons, including "three-fifths of all other persons."

Without a trial by jury the status of an alleged fugitive could be decided by a circuit judge or any state magistrate.

The fourth major event respecting slavery during these forty years was the legal termination of the foreign slave trade on January 1, 1808, by an act of Congress passed the preceding March. Even so the acquisition and transporting of slaves was so lucrative that it was not wholly suppressed.

As slavery first came under the critical scrutiny of moralists the typical slave holder tried to react dispassionately by maintaining that actual conditions were not as objectionable as claimed by outside observers. When the condemnation of slavery reached the point where the relationship between master and slave was everywhere and in all cases designated as a sin per se, then southerners "began to construct a moral philosophy under which slavery could be authoritatively supported."[2]

In *An Essay on Slavery* by Thomas Roderick Dew, President of William and Mary College in Virginia, the writer contended that slavery was as old as the human race, and had been an accepted social institution of the Chosen People. Thus it is undeniably a "necessary result of the laws of mind and matter," indicating "some benevolent design" and "intended by our Creator for some useful purpose." To be specific, it reduces the number of wars by attaching primitive men and tribes to a sedentary society; it equips savages, who are naturally lazy, for useful work, and elevates them far above any standard of living they could ever have attained if they had not been rescued from their backward state. America's "share in the original sin by which slavery was first introduced into this country" is minimized and the blame assigned to the British who did not discourage the slave traffic.[3]

By 1840 it is estimated that of the 2,700,000 slaves in America, 80,000 were members of the Methodist Church, 80,000 were

[2] William Sumner Jenkins, *Pro-Slavery Thought in the Old South* (Chapel Hill, N. C.: University of North Carolina Press, 1935), p. 200.

[3] John R. Bodo, *The Protestant Clergy and Public Issues, 1812-1848* (Princeton: Princeton University Press, 1954), pp. 134, 135.

Baptist, and about 40,000 belonged to other denominations. All slave owners had been excluded from the Quaker fellowship by this time. The acrimonious dispute over slavery among Methodists resulted in an open rupture along sectional lines which was not healed until the 1930's.[4] Applying their strong emphasis on separation of church and state, Baptists called slavery "a question purely of political economy, and one which in this country is reserved to the cognizance of the state governments severally. . . ." The function of religion is only to prescribe the reciprocal duties in the slave-master interrelationship. The Charleston Association of the Baptist Church addressed a memorial to the legislature of South Carolina with the avowed opinion that the Divine Author of Christianity did not think it desirable to interfere with the existing institution of slavery:

> The right of the master to dispose of the time of his slaves has been distinctly recognized by the Creator of all things, who is surely at liberty to vest the right of property over any subject in whomsoever He pleases.[5]

Prophetic judgments on the culpability of the churches were not lacking. Parker Pillsbury, as one zealot for righteousness, charged that ecclesiastical endorsement was the strongest bulwark that slavery could boast:

> Let it be driven from the Church, with the burning zeal of its reprobation and execration stamped on its iron brow, and its fate is fixed forever. Only while its horrors are baptized and sanctified in the name of Christianity, can it maintain an existence. . . . Our religion has been found at war with the interests of humanity and the laws of God. And it is more than time the world was awakened to its

[4] A concise account of the "Slavery Controversy and Schisms" in major American denominations is given by William Warren Sweet, *The Story of Religion in America* (New York: Harper, 1950), pp. 285-311.

[5] Leonard L. Haynes, Jr., *The Negro Community within American Protestantism, 1619-1844* (Boston: Christopher, 1953), p. 185.

unhallowed influence on the hopes and happiness of man, while it makes itself the palladium of the foulest iniquity ever perpetrated in the sight of heaven.[6]

Under the pressure of criticism from the northern moralists, southern apologists undertook exhaustive research to compile a scriptural defense of slavery. In the pre-Civil War era, except for rare circles of freethinkers who were regarded as outside the pale of Christianity, the divine inspiration and infallibility of the Bible were taken for granted. Thus, much of the controversy between abolitionists and slaveholders, or to be more exact, between their clerical spokesmen, was based on their respective interpretations of Scripture. The vital issue to be decided, as far as they were concerned, was whether slavery was actually sanctioned by the Old Testament and permitted by the New as southerners insisted, or whether it was a flat violation of the precepts of the gospel as some northerners maintained. With energetic determination the theologians of the South turned to a study of the Bible to bolster their position and counterattack their opponents. Southern representatives in Congress frequently alluded to the teachings of the Bible as one of their most effective tactics in sectional debates.

In 1856 the correspondence between two prominent divines, the Reverend Richard Fuller of Beaufort, South Carolina, and the Reverend Francis Wayland of Providence, Rhode Island, was published under the heading of "Domestic Slavery Considered as a Scriptural Institution." Dr Fuller reaffirmed the basic position of the southern Christian in capital letters: WHAT GOD SANCTIONED IN THE OLD TESTAMENT AND PERMITTED IN THE NEW CANNOT BE SIN, and clinched his argument by quoting the familiar proof text: "All Scripture is given by inspiration of God" (II Tim. 3:16). According to this interpretation abolitionist opinions were doctrinal heresy. Biblical infallibility im-

[6] Parker Pillsbury, *The Church As It Is or the Forlorn Hope of Slavery* (Boston: Bela Marsh, 1847), p. 3. The book prints extracts from the pronouncements of churches and clergy.

plied the permissibility of slavery. Northerners were tampering with the unalterable decrees of God when they arrogated to themselves the right to adjust the Christian message to fit changing circumstances. Repudiating certain biblical pronouncements as obsolete when they do not appeal to us is a precarious procedure, warned the southern churchman. To say that slavery is at variance with the New Testament, is to make the Bible contradict itself and undermine its inerrancy. Where northern theologians have gone astray, Dr. Fuller maintained, is in putting their human calculations above biblical affirmations, as though we have "outgrown the childish ignorance and simplicity of the apostles."[7]

Southern apologetics started with the premise that the moral law is immutable. What was not blameworthy at one stage of human history cannnot be denounced now. It would be impious to suggest that God at any time, under any conditions, gave his express approval to something which was unjust. Jesus emphatically declared that he came to fulfill the Law and not to abolish it. Therefore, whatever happened under the Old Covenant must have met with his approval. Slavery has flourished in every part of the world and has never been catalogued as one of the sins which Christians must avoid. Did not Christ tacitly approve it when he healed the slave of the Roman officer while he issued no edict of emancipation (Luke 7:2-10)? Did the apostles not teach the submission and obedience of slaves to their masters and exhort them to be content with their lot (cf. Col. 3:22; Eph. 6:5-8; I Pet. 2:18)? The relation between master and slave is not intrinsically and invariably wicked. In the apostolic writings it is treated in the same context and on the same footing with the relation existing between parent and child or husband and wife. To be sure, God has circumscribed these natural relationships with specific regulations which must be observed, but slavery in itself is no more evil than marriage or the family. Pointing to the epistle to Philemon it was urged that St.

[7] Richard Fuller and Francis Weyland, *Domestic Slavery Considered as a Scriptural Institution* (New York: Sheldon, Lamport and Blakeman, 1856), pp. 170-72. Cf. p. 210.

Paul's method of handling Onesimus clearly demonstrates that it is our Christian obligation to apprehend runaway slaves and restore them to their masters.[8]

One of the favorite biblical sources for southern writers was the Mosaic code which authorized the buying, selling, holding, and bequeathing of slaves as property. The only restriction was that fellow Israelites were not to be enslaved (cf. Lev. 25:44-46). It was noted that the Levitical law was applied by Joshua when he made the conquered Gibeonites "hewers of wood and drawers of water" (Josh. 9:27).

Christian slaveholders were taught to think of their situation as a continuation of the patriarchal system in which slaves were a part of the household. Just as the head of the household was responsible for supervising the upbringing of his children so he should exercise a benevolent discipline toward his slaves. The planters who were looking for biblical precedent viewed themselves as nineteenth-century successors to Abraham and Jacob.[9]

The favorite argument used by those seeking a religious sanction for slavery was to refer to the curse which Noah pronounced on his grandson Canaan: "A slave of slaves shall he be to his brothers. . . . Blessed by the Lord my God be Shem; and let Canaan be his slave. God enlarge Japheth, and let him dwell in the tents of Shem; and let Canaan be his slave" (cf. Gen. 9:25-27). One southern commentator saw in the discovery and conquest of America the means by which God enlarged the tents of Japheth:

> No sooner did Japheth begin to enlarge himself, and to dwell in the tents of Shem, than Canaan left his fastnesses in the wilds of Africa where the white man's foot had never trod, and appeared on the beach to get passage to America, as if drawn thither by an

[8] An Old Testament parallel was found in the story of the escaped slave Hagar who was commanded to return to her mistress Sarah (Gen. 16:9).

[9] Bishop Elliott of Georgia, with the patriarchal prototype in mind could say on the eve of the Civil War that "we are fighting to protect and preserve a race who form a part of our household and stand with us next to our children." (Sermon, Christ Church, Savannah, 1861.) Quoted in Jenkins, *op. cit.*, p. 210.

impulse of his nature to fulfill his destiny of becoming Japheth's servant.[10]

Was it hypocrisy or self-delusion when Jefferson Davis used this same rationale for slavery in a speech delivered to the Democratic state convention in Jackson, Mississippi, in 1859?[11] Since it was difficult to establish a connecting link between the curse and the Negro race a kind of speculative etymology was used to assist. Dr. S. A. Cartwright tried to show that biblical names were all prophetic. Accordingly Ham means "the progenitor of hot and black" and Canaan meant "the self-submissive kneebender."[12]

Southern churchmen found a partial answer to the drastic humanitarian demand for liberation in a renewed effort to evangelize and educate the Negroes during the 1820's and 1830's. Idealists who could not "turn traitor" to "the southern way of life" wanted to believe that it would be possible to remove the most objectionable abuses without abolishing the system. The clergy of the South were almost unanimous in opposing any proposal to reopen the slave trade.[13] Ironically enough there is considerable evidence to substantiate the claim of southern ministers that they were doing more for the Christian instruction of slaves than their critics were doing in the North for the freemen. A Presbyterian minister in North Carolina recommended a constructive outlet for the "exuberant compassion" of the enemies of slavery: They could send financial support for the southern sponsored undertaking of bringing the gospel to the enslaved Africans.[14] Another taunt which southerners hurled at their self-righteous foes was to remind them of the miser-

[10] S. A. Cartwright in *Essays* (Natchez, 1843), pp. 7, 8: "being inductions from the Baconian philosophy proving the truth of the Bible and the justice and benevolence of the decree dooming Canaan to be a servant of servants." Quoted in Jenkins, *op. cit.*, p. 205.

[11] ". . . the good Bishop Las Casas with philosophical humanity inaugurated the importation of the race of Ham." Quoted in Jenkins, *op. cit.*, p. 205.

[12] Jenkins, *op. cit.*, p. 206. [13] Cf. *Ibid.*, pp. 211-18.

[14] Cf. Bodo, *op. cit.*, pp. 145-47.

able hovels into which freed Negroes of the North were shunted and confined.[15]

How oblivious some gentlemen scholars could be to grim realities is seen in the wishful thinking of a man like Beverley Tucker[16] who averred that slavery was favorable to the inculcation of religion in both master and slaves. Sure signs of Christian influence could be seen "in the cheerful humility, the liberal obedience, the devoted loyalty of the slave, and in the gentleness, the kindness, the courtesy of the master."[17]

To gain a comprehensive understanding of the theological controversy over slavery it is necessary to be aware of the more inflexible orthodoxy of the South in comparison to the liberalization of theology in some northern seminaries. The changing philosophical climate in New England included the intrusion of German rationalism which induced the more open-minded theologians to adopt a more critical view of the Bible. At least some southern clergymen looked upon Harvard and Yale as hotbeds of religious infidelity, inevitably interwoven with political radicalism.[18] One justification for southern secession came to be the alleged moral necessity of separating from a regime which was pervaded with rationalistic and atheistic principles.

[15] A similar defense mechanism is seen today when southerners remind northerners of the racial conflict and discrimination persisting in northern urban centers.

[16] Beverley Tucker was a Virginian who moved to Missouri to make his fortune. Later he taught law at William and Mary. A defender of states rights and an advocate of secession, his political and economic creed included a hatred of central government, tariff, democracy, and the Yankee brand of industrialism, while he loved agrarianism and the "happy darky." In a speech in 1850 Tucker declared: "God forbid that I would desire to introduce slavery [in Ohio]. . . . I would not so wrong the Negro. He is proud and happy in his subordination to one worthy to be his master. But servitude under such as these . . . would break his heart. . . . The man of Ohio has nobody below him but his hog." See Nathaniel Beverley Tucker, *The Partisan Leader,* ed. Carl Bridenbaugh (New York: Knopf, 1933), p. xxiv.

[17] Jenkins, *op. cit.,* p. 226.

[18] Cf. the present day attack of some "Bible belt" fundamentalists on integration, modernism, evolution, and communism. To their way of thinking these are all inseparable evils with a Satanic origin.

The South Carolina divine, Richard Fuller, countered northern moralists by reminding them of embarrassing historical facts. Southerners had not inaugurated the slave trade. Sometimes the importations of laborers from Africa were imposed upon the colonies despite their protests, he averred. The commerce was instigated by English and northern speculators. Once a vessel was freighted with human cargo there was only one alternative for the Negro—"deliverance from his loathsome dungeon by the planter." Otherwise the wretched captives could only suffer in protracted agony until relieved by death.[19] In this attempted rebuttal of indignant northerners, the southerner was placating his conscience with the assumption that he was relatively compassionate in accepting the responsibility of slave holding which had been thrust upon him contrary to his wishes by the criminal scheming of outsiders. The Yankees and the British should be damned for the plight in which he found himself! Instead they were acting like pious hypocrites. While the argument was scarcely tenable it should have been disturbing enough to have prevented northern Christians from concluding that their hands were clean of the whole mess that was defiling the nation. A hundred and more years later the same sectional disputes arouse rancor on both sides. Who is most guilty in the abuse of the Negro? Condescending southerners who pride themselves in their benign treatment of inferiors point a finger of scorn at self-righteous northerners who shut Negroes into the ghettoes of their cities and evade all personal contact with them. "Liberation" above the Mason-Dixon line has deprived the Negro of the warm personal regard for his welfare displayed by benefactors in the South.

In his letters to Prof. Weyland in Rhode Island, Dr. Fuller observed that slavery was upheld "by men of the most devoted piety and exalted philanthropy." Reflecting the fears proceeding from his own aristocratic frame of mind he reminded his correspondent of the frightful consequences of an "immediate and unconditional

[19] Fuller and Weyland, *op. cit.,* p. 131.

abolition." The prevailing social structures would be overthrown. A devastating revolution would bring ruination to the entire South. "Irreparable mischief" would be inflicted on the slaves themselves who were utterly unprepared for liberty and would only seize upon it as a license for indolence and crime. Inevitably it would transform them

> from a contented and cheerful peasantry, into a horde of outlaws, a multitude of paupers with whom the white population could never amalgamate, who must forever feel themselves . . . degraded and outcast from the kindred and privileges of the superior caste; who, deprived of the master's protection, and no longer bound to their governors by the kindly and almost filial ties now existing, would endure perpetual humiliation and insult.[20]

One of the most influential and intellectually competent defenses of slavery was made by the venerated Dr. James Henley Thornwell, professor of theology at the Presbyterian seminary in Columbia, South Carolina. Appealing to the widespread loyalty to the Scriptures that still predominated among clergy and laity alike, he presented the subject in such a way that slavery and the Bible seemed to stand or fall together. Concurring fully with his fellow South Carolinian, Dr. Fuller, he contended that abolitionism is refuted by the authority of the divine word. Northern moralists tend to deny the sufficiency and plenary inspiration of the Holy Book. To make any concessions which would allow for a "defective morality in the Bible" is to encourage a spirit of godless rationalism. Opposition to slavery, according to Thornwell, has never been grounded in the sacred writings of the Christian church. It has arisen "from visionary theories of human nature and society." When northern extremists condemn slavery "they are striking at the foundation of our common faith."[21]

[20] *Ibid.*, p. 136.

[21] James Henley Thornwell, "Relation of the Church to Slavery," *Collected Writings* (Richmond: Presbyterian Committee of Publication, 1873), IV, 393.

The church, Thornwell argued, dare not disturb a relation which the Bible approves. The question is not whether masters are acceptable in the Christian communion, but "whether those who exclude them should not themselves be rejected."[22] The southern churches do not demand that their brethren in Europe or in the northern states introduce slavery. They grant them the freedom to choose whatever economic system is in their best interest. They only plead that outsiders refrain from passing judgment on a way of life that has proven successful and desirable in the South.

Meanwhile Christian masters should be alerted to their responsibilities for the spiritual welfare of their slaves. Displaying the typical paternalistic attitude of the benevolent-minded southerner, Thornwell admonished his readers not to neglect the religious instruction of slaves. Enlightened self-interest, he assumes, will induce the planters to provide the physical necessities of life. Unaware of the scientific claim that will be made by anthropology and psychology at a later date, he was fully a child of his own age in proceeding on the supposition of innate racial inferiority. Negroes should not be entrusted with the spiritual leadership of their own people. Even the most enlightened among them are prone "to superstition and extravagance."[23]

On May 26, 1850, James Henley Thornwell delivered an oft-quoted sermon before an assembly comprising the most distinguished citizens of Charleston, preaching on the text, "Masters, give unto your servants that which is just and equal; knowing that you also have a Master in heaven" (Col. 4:1). The occasion was the dedication of a new edifice for the worship and religious education of colored people. Hailing the completion of the building as a monument to the Christian philanthropy of southern gentlemen, the Presbyterian theologian seems to be forecasting the day when

[22] *Ibid.*, p. 386, cf. p. 388: "He who would debar a slaveholder from the table of the Lord . . . deserves himself to be excluded for usurping the prerogatives of Christ."

[23] *Ibid.*, pp. 396-97.

separate (but unequal) facilities will be provided for Negroes to preserve the caste system while assuaging the consciences of professing Christians. There is only one string attached by the "good people of Charleston" in the use of their generous gift. Only a *safe* version of Christianity is to be taught. "The name of Jesus is not a name for conspirators to conjure with—it carries no danger with it." The new church is to be an added safeguard "against insubordination and rebellion."[24]

With clarity of style and an eloquence of speech that would excel most northern orators of the period, Thornwell extolled the munificence of the southern aristocracy and sought to refute the monstrous "misrepresentations which ignorance, malice, and fanaticism are constantly and assiduously propagating."[25] His denunciations of misguided zealots who are stirring up discontent are likely to remind us of the frantic efforts of southern extremists in our own day to discredit the Southern Christian Leadership Conference, the NAACP, or CORE as dangerous in their agitation, if not communist inspired and controlled. "The parties in conflict are not merely Abolitionists and Slaveholders; they are Atheists, Socialists, Communists, Red Republicans, Jacobins on the one side, and friends of order and regulated freedom on the other."[26]

Thornwell anticipates eventual divine vindication for the southern cause. Sensitive to the attack on slavery as anti-Christian he pleaded for moderation among his fellow southerners. The kind treatment of slaves will help remove the opprobrium that many Christians have attached to the retention of the slavery system. His repeated concern that they must "stand acquitted at the bar of God" seemed to betray his own misgivings and doubts as to the righteousness of their cause.

The political philosophy of John Calhoun is reflected in the theologian's claim

[24] Cf. "The Christian Doctrine of Slavery," *ibid.*, p. 398 ff.

[25] *Ibid.*, p. 400.

[26] *Ibid.*, p. 405.

> that the very principles upon which we have been accustomed to justify Southern slavery are the principles of regulated liberty . . . we have been supporting representative, republican government against the despotism of masses on the one hand, and the supremacy of a single will on the other.[27]

Thornwell was chagrined by the "misapprehension" of Dr. Channing that slavery annuls all human and personal rights by treating men as property. In his retort he relied on proof texts from St. Paul in which the apostle speaks of the services of slaves as duties. A moral obligation is implied which could not be affirmed in "the mechanical employment of instruments and things." The power which the master exerts "is a right, not to the *man,* but to his *labor"* (emphasis Thornwell's). The basic distinction between free and slave labor is "that one is rendered in consequence of a contract; the other is rendered in consequence of a command." The punishments that are inflicted for the disobedience of a slave are analogous to the penalties imposed by the law for breaches of contract. "All that is necessary . . . is that the punishment should be just." Pain wrongly inflicted "is cruelty, whether that cruelty springs from the tyranny of a single master or the tyranny of that greater master, the state."[28]

In his vindication of the slavery system Thornwell forgets that according to his own orthodox theology which stresses natural depravity it is precarious to place too much power in the hands of a special interest group. Whenever anyone has unrestrained control over the life and activity of another human being he is prone to abuse it. Granting the suppositions of traditional Presbyterian doctrine regarding the sinfulness of human nature, it could have been foreseen that the extension of slavery would lead to corruption and the most abhorrent cruelties. The rejoinder to Thornwell's use of New Testament injunctions would be to point out that St. Paul, confronted by the grim reality of a slave society and looking for-

[27] *Ibid.,* p. 404.
[28] *Ibid.,* pp. 408-15.

ward to the early reappearance of Christ, sought to mitigate the evils of the prevalent system for the interim period. He did this by reminding the master that he too stood under the judgment of the Supreme Master and was accountable to him for the way in which he discharged his responsibilities. The problem of what should be done if the master feels no sense of responsibility to God is left unanswered.

One way in which the orthodox theology typified by Thornwell sought to straddle the moral issues involved in slavery was to shift the focus of attention into the spiritual realm and deliver a diatribe against the bondage to sin. The words of Jesus were recalled: "Whoever commits sin is the slave of sin." Thornwell drew on his thorough training in the classics to quote from Seneca, Pythagoras, Cicero, and Plato to show that these ancient writers agreed that a person of wealth or noble birth could be as much of a slave to passion or greed as the impoverished and dispossessed.

> The monarch on his throne . . . may be . . . despicable in the sight of the holy and the good, while the poor slave, in his humble hovel, or on his pallet of straw, may possess a dignity and moral grandeur which assert his affinity with heaven.[29]

There is an inward freedom which Christ gained through his redemptive activity that is available for the slave as well as the master. Neither chains nor imprisonment can deprive an individual of the liberty which God bestows upon the believer. When the slave renders service to his master out of obedience to God it is "free service." Thus it can even be said that "involuntary servitude" is a sin on the part of the slave, not on the part of the master who must demand it. But willing submission and eager service for their overlords may "fit them for thrones in the kingdom of God."[30]

It is not difficult to understand why Thornwell was in favor with the southern aristocracy. While there is no reason to question his

[29] *Ibid.*, pp. 417-19.
[30] *Ibid.*

sincerity, he ingratiated himself with the ruling class by adapting the whole structure of his theology to an *apologia* for the continuation of slavery. Like his segregationist descendants in our day, he helped to salve the conscience of the Christian community. The Marxist caricature of Christianity is reflected by his disregard for the untold sufferings of the slaves which he refers to as "the defective arrangement of the details,"[31] and by his repeated promise of a kind of "pie in the sky when you die."

In full agreement with traditional Christianity, Thornwell conceded that in the final consummation all distinctions between people will be dissolved. "There will be no bondage in heaven."[32] God's eventual objective is the perfection of humanity. If it had not been for the transgression of Adam there would have been full equality in an earthly paradise. Echoing the explanation of the early Church Fathers, this theologian of the South called slavery the curse of sin. He admitted that slavery is fundamentally evil and out of harmony with the Christian ideal. But it is precisely at this point that he found a heresy in the writings of the liberal churchmen of the North. "The Gospel does not propose to make our present state a perfect one—to make our earth a heaven." Our fallen world requires gradations in social rank to promote enterprise and industry. As the races have developed under the providence of God, the free citizens of England or America "could not endure the condition of African bondage." But governments must be conformed to the needs of their people "and subjection to a master" may be the means by which the culturally and intellectually inferior Negro "is most effectually trained to the moral end of his being." Slavery may be at least a relative good; although founded on a curse, God in his goodness extracts from it a blessing. In some imperfect societies it may be essential for the well-being of the majority.[33]

[31] *Ibid.*, p. 415. [32] *Ibid.*, p. 419. Cf. p. 430: "The slave may be fitted in his humble and . . . degraded lot for shining as a star in the firmament of heaven."
[33] Cf. *ibid.*, pp. 419-24.

(Apparently it never occurred to the intellectuals of the South that the simple use of a color line in separating the competent from the incompetent was a most unscientific way of determining talent. How much potential genius was suppressed by enforced servitude and lack of opportunity is as impossible to estimate as it was an irreparable loss to the nation.)

Thornwell was indignant in his rebuttal of the accusation that the South was violating the golden rule by treating Africans in a way which they would resent if the roles were reversed. Such a strictly literal interpretation, he counters, would not allow the judge to condemn the criminal nor the rich man to claim his possessions. Actually "the precept is simply the inculcation of justice from the motives of love." What we are required to do is to handle our slaves in a manner that would be just "if we were slaves ourselves." This was a sufficiently cautious presentation of the New Testament imperative of love that any slaveholder could afford to nod his assent.[34]

Thornwell strains his theological ingenunity to provide props for the preservation of the privileged classes. The hardships that are sometimes heaped upon the slaves are at least partially compensated for by carefree existence without the burdens of responsibility borne by the owners. The Negroes are not to be excluded from th "spiritual" benefits of Christianity. The Presbyterian professor was a staunch advocate of Christian training for the slaves, which he was confident would make them more dependable and honest. Thus he assures the slaveholders that their financial investment in this worthy undertaking would not only help silence the abolitionist agitators, but it would also be rewarded with more conscientious service from their workers. Unlike the proponents of apartheid in the Union of South Africa, who passed the Bantu Education Act to assure the training of natives for perpetual servitude, Thornwell did not fear Christian influence but contended that it would foster contentment and help eradicate revolutionary sentiment.

[34] Cf. *ibid.*, pp. 428, 429.

> Our highest security in these states lies in the confidence and affection of our servants. . . . Brutal ignorance is indeed to be dreaded. . . . But Christian knowledge softens and subdues.[35]

Anachronistic as much of Thornwell's argumentation must strike the modern reader it is not by any means completely passé. After the Civil War his writings were collected and printed. During reconstruction days they were used to vindicate the past record of the South and to help formulate a religious basis for the segregation of the races. Among the Dutch Reformed in South Africa, where an orthdox brand of Calvinism is still promulgated, rationalizations similar to those of Thornwell are often repeated.[36] However, for the most part, at least the theological leaders among southern Presbyterians have repudiated racism, and the official pronouncements of the assembly of the Presbyterian Church in the U. S. (South) have called for the elimination of all forms of discrimination.

At the same time, White Citizens Councils are able to find compliant clergy who will serve as chaplains for their meetings. Especially among some of the Southern Baptists, and among the more militant fundamentalist and Pentecostal bodies, the Bible is still used as a source book for upholding segregation. The pastor of a large Baptist church in Dallas distributed a sermon which he preached in answer to the Supreme Court decision of 1954 entitled "God the Original Segregationist." Moses, Jesus, and Paul are all represented as people who would be unalterably opposed to any mingling of the races. The curse pronounced by Noah after the Genesis deluge is given a new twist to adapt it to the changed situation in the South. Not all the Negro descendants of Ham but only the fraction in the line of his son Canaan have been condemned to servitude. If all colored were ordained to be servants of whites, segregation of the races would be impractical.[37]

[35] *Ibid.*, p. 435. [36] Cf. David M. Paton, *Church and Race in South Africa* (London: SCM Press, 1958), pp. 94-103.

[37] Carey Daniel in sermon published by Bible Book Store (Dallas, 1955).

Thornwell and his colleagues might be appalled to find that their mantle has fallen on diehard segregationists of mediocre ability. Yet the main threads of the theological defense of slavery crystalized in the ante-bellum era are still discernible in the thinking of clergy and laity in the 1960's who want to be loyal to the "southern way of life." An Episcopal rector like the Reverend James P. Dees of Statesville, North Carolina, could reassemble all the stock biblical arguments on a shallow level that would have seemed unworthy to a cultured gentleman like Thornwell, but the parallels are unmistakable. As slavery was once deemed to be part of the created order, so now segregation is in accord with the divine will. Thornwell could maintain that slavery would promote the Negro's welfare. Dees can assert that segregation is in the best interest of both races. The pre-Civil War theologian could sound the alarm about Marxist and atheistic influences among the radicals of the North. Dees can uncover communist infiltration in the National Association for the Advancement of Colored People and the National Council of Churches.[38]

The theological controversy over slavery has abated, but we have lived to witness its recrudescence under a new guise.

[38] Cf. James P. Dees, "A Survey of the Racial Issue," *The Defender* (November, 1958), pp. 28-32.

5 The Theological Protest Against Slavery

The more aggressive southerners became in their approbation of slavery, the more vehement northerners became in their campaign against it. As the sectional rift deepened, anti-slavery advocates left the South and provided more ammunition for the arsenal of the abolitionists. Opinion ranged all the way from mild criticism of slavery to the violent attacks of William Lloyd Garrison calling for immediate emancipation and open defiance of constitutional law. Garrison, in the judgment of his most recent biographer, was responsible for the atmosphere of moral absolutism which incited the Civil War and eventuated in the liberation of the slaves. For him abolition became equivalent to a fiery religion in which he repudiated all suggestions of expediency or compromise, developed an apocalyptic view of the world, and projected a form of Christian perfectionism.[1] His most famous editorial appeared in the fourth issue of the *Liberator:*

> I will be as harsh as truth, and as uncompromising as justice, . . . I am in earnest—I will not equivocate—I will not excuse—I will not retreat a single inch—AND I WILL BE HEARD.

There were other voices that sounded more moderate, but em-

[1] Cf. John L. Thomas, *The Liberator: William Lloyd Garrison* (New York: Little, Brown and Co., 1963).

phatic enough. In 1837 Theodore Weld, who became an abolitionist lobbyist in Washington, authored a widely read and distributed treatise called *The Bible Against Slavery* with the informative subtitle "an inquiry into the patriarchal and Mosaic systems on the subject of human rights." In his analysis slavery is found to be contrary to the commandments, "Thou shalt not steal" and "Thou shalt not covet." Slavery is the worst kind of theft because it steals the whole person. Slaveholders covet Negroes for the evil purposes of exploitation, ostentation, and sensual gratification.[2]

Encountering southern biblicists on their own field of battle, Weld strains the exegesis of passages in Leviticus and Deuteronomy to demonstrate that servitude as practiced by the Israelites was not a prototype for American slavery. Persons became servants voluntarily. They were compensated for their labor. There was no sharp class cleavage; master and "slave" worked together. Never were servants treated as legal property, but had definite rights including the privilege of worship and rest on the Sabbath.[3]

Beriah Green, professor of Sacred Literature at Western Reserve, whose collected sermons ran into a third edition, was another northerner who used biblical exposition to undermine the case for slavery.[4] The Reverend LaRoy Sutherland, a Methodist revival preacher, laboriously indexed almost every Bible verse which might be construed as related to the issue of slavery.

The suggestion that the black skin of the Negro was the mark of Cain was met by the abolitionist counterargument that the posterity of Cain were all drowned in the deluge. The favorite theory of southerners that Negroes were under the curse which Noah had pronounced on Canaan was refuted in various ways. Some questioned the genealogy demanding proof that the Africans were really the offspring of Canaan. The usual explanation of the bibli-

[2] Theodore Weld, *The Bible Against Slavery* (New York: American Anti-Slavery Society, 1837), pp. 9-11.

[3] *Ibid.*, pp. 22-46.

[4] E.g., Beriah Green, *Slavery not in the New Testament and the Chattel Principle, the Abhorrence of Jesus Christ and the Apostles* (New York: American Anti-Slavery Society, 1839).

cally oriented abolitionists was that Noah was uttering a prophecy of what would happen, not a command for southern planters to execute. By analogy, it was pointed out, the prophecies of Christ's death do not justify his murderers.[5]

A good deal of printer's ink was used to explain how the early Hebrews could have practiced slavery. In patriarchal days it was alleged that servitude was voluntary. Poor men often sold themselves as servants. Besides, how could Abraham have led 318 armed servants on a military expedition to rescue his nephew Lot if they were comparable in status to Negro slaves? John Rankin even proposed the romantic thought that "Abraham, being benevolent as well as rich, made a practice of redeeming miserable captives of war who then rendered him willing and voluntary service." Others approached the issue by saying that if the example of Abraham could be used to justify slavery, then lying and concubinage (which are also recorded) should be sanctioned.[6]

The Jews, according to abolitionist theory, were the select people of God in a unique situation. They were God's chosen instruments in meting out punishment against the "seven nations" whose abominable transgressions evoked God's wrath (Deut. 7). This limited permission for slavery, at a particular time under carefully circumscribed conditions, does not justify the imposition or retention of slavery in the nineteenth century.

> When the slaveholders of the present day have obtained of the same Author of Rights a *license* [emphasis his] to deal in the bodies and souls of men, then, and not till then, will we admit any comparison of Hebrew bondage with American slavery.[7]

Repeatedly it was mentioned by the Bible-conscious abolitionists that servitude in the Old Testament, even the epoch of Egyptian

[5] Weld, *op. cit.,* pp. 46-48, uses both of these counterarguments.

[6] Cf. Shanks, "The Biblical Anti-Slavery Argument," *The Journal of Negro History,* XVI, 138, 139.

[7] Address of the Starksborough and Lincoln Anti-Slavery Society, pp. 7, 8. Quoted by Shanks, *op. cit.,* p. 140.

bondage, was much more mild and merciful than the abhorrent slavery system endorsed by many southern Christians.

Other abolitionists with Christian convictions did not attempt to explain and excuse the slavery prevalent among the Hebrews. In an address to the Yale alumni in 1843, Horace Bushnell characterized the Mosaic ordinances as "permissive statutes" which had no permanent significance and were to be superseded by the evolution of higher laws. Slavery was subject to elimination by the progressive growth of moral sentiment.[8]

More literalistic interpreters of the Bible observed that ten plagues were inflicted on the Egyptians for enslaving God's people. By contrast Cyrus, the Persian king, was blessed for emancipating the Jewish exiles. The prophet Obed denounced the reprisal of the northern kingdom of Israel in seizing fellow Hebrews as slaves, and demanded the restoration of the 200,000 captives (II Chron. 28:8-15). Jeremiah and Nehemiah, it was noted, sternly rebuked the Jews for allowing slavery (cf. Jer. 34:8-22; Neh. 5:5 ff.). Tyre, which seems to have been a center for the ancient slave trade, was the object of fiery prophetic malediction.[9]

Within the framework of a rigid biblical theology abolitionist exegetes faced a more arduous task in accommodating the New Testament to their crusade. Under Roman law slaves were regarded as personal property to be used according to the whims of their masters. Atrocities were common. Tacitus records the infamous case of Pedanius Secundus who had four hundred of his slaves slain because their master was found murdered and no one person had confessed the crime. Jesus and the apostles seemed to take the existing social order for granted and said nothing in outright condemnation of this monstrous system.

Unimpressed and undaunted, Bible-believing abolitionists entered the logomachy. The Greek word *doulos,* they argued, does not necessarily mean "slave." It would be better translated in most in-

[8] Cf. Shanks, *op. cit.,* p. 143. [9] Cf. *ibid.,* p. 146.

stances as "servant." The duties inculcated in servants in the Pauline epistles connoted a reciprocity of benefits. Onesimus, the "runaway slave" who fled to St. Paul for counsel, was to be readmitted into the service of Philemon as a real Christian brother. The apostle hinted that the Corinthian slaves who were converted to Christianity should take advantage of any opportunity they might have for freedom (I Cor. 7:21). Understandably enough, slavery was not anathematized directly, because Christians were a minority group trying to disseminate their message as widely as possible. An accusation of instigating a slave uprising against the Roman government would jeopardize their mission to "make disciples of all nations." Under the prevailing circumstances the early Christian leaders were persuaded that it was in the best interest of the "slaves" themselves to encourage them to remain where they were and not attempt a futile revolt. The eschatological consciousness which pervaded the first Christian communities strengthened them to endure momentary distress while awaiting eternal bliss.[10]

Among the zealots for abolition was George B. Cheever who spoke of "God's wrath against slavery," "ruin of a nation," and "the throne of iniquity" which should be expelled from the fellowship of Christians. He denied that the Hebrews actually practiced slavery—incontrovertibly it was a damnable sin because it was incompatible with the law of love and unsupported by biblical precedents. Pointing to the "sacredness of parental relations" he maintained that slavery identical with "man-stealing" was a direct violation of God's will concerning the human family. Since the Hebrews were forbidden to restore runaway slaves the American law pertaining to the restoration of fugitives was unbiblical. The testimony of Jeremiah and Ezekiel, together with the "Jubilee Statute of Universal Freedom," was invoked to heap coals of fire on "the peculiar institution" that was demoralizing America.[11]

[10] Cf. *ibid.*, pp. 148-50. [11] Cf. the chapter titles in George B. Cheever, *God Against Slavery: and the Freedom and Duty of the Pulpit to Rebuke It as a Sin against God* (Cincinnati: American Reform Tract and Book Society, n.d.).

Cheever thundered a furious diatribe against the "ludicrous and wicked" suggestion that Africans could be held as property by reason of the curse recorded in Genesis:

> For in the first place, it was not God, but Noah, who pronounced the curse; in the second place, the curse fell not upon Ham, but upon Canaan, whose descendants were as white as the Hebrews or ourselves; in the third place the descendants of Ham, as you claim the Africans to be, have nothing to do with this curse . . . .[12]

To claim a "charter from heaven" to be God's ministers of vengeance upon a whole continent of men was castigated by Cheever as "the wildest, vastest, most sweeping and diabolical forgery ever conceived or committed." Waxing hot with anger, he demands to know:

> Where is the sentence in which God ever appointed you, the Anglo-Saxon race, you, the mixture of all races under heaven, you, who cannot tell whether the blood of Shem, Ham, or Japhet mingles in your veins, you, the assertors of a right to traffic in human flesh, you, . . . by this very claim, more degraded, more debased in your moral principles, than the lowest tribe of Jews who were swept for their sins from the promised land. Where is the sentence in which God ever appointed you, four thousand years after Noah and his children had gone to their graves in peace, to be the executors of Noah's will, with the whole inheritance given to you, as your property, for your profit, the reward of your faithfulness in fulfilling God's curse?[13]

Another leading antagonist of slavery was Albert Barnes, a Philadelphia divine, who was worried about its disruptive influence on the Union and believed it was a duty incumbent upon every Christian to expose the evils of the vicious institution. Crossing swords with southern churchmen on the biblical field of battle he contended that they were abusing Holy Writ when they appealed to it in their pro-slavery apologetics. Argument by argument he countered with his own scriptural evidence. As for the Old Testament,

[12] *Ibid.,* p. 100. [13] *Ibid.,* pp. 100-101.

he claimed that "it would have been as just for the Egyptians to retain the Hebrews in bondage, as it is for white America to retain the African race."[14]

Among the more liberal churchmen who deplored the excesses of the abolitionists, but who nonetheless found slavery repugnant, was William Ellery Channing. His broad humane outlook caused him to sympathize as much with the slaves as he did with any victims of persecution or tyranny. Without declaring Scripture obsolete or irrelevant he used a more rational approach to unsettle the apologists for the slavery system. With a firm faith in "the everlasting law of rectitude" he regarded the question of slavery as primarily a moral issue. Incitement to revolution, attacks on the constitution, and dangers to the solidarity of the union were dreaded as much by him as by any other lover of good order and peace. Only the prodigious moral harm perpetrated by the persistence of slavery could motivate him to write against it.

Channing objected to reducing human beings with their natural rights and inborn dignity to chattel. "It is iniquitous to seize a man and hold him as property because he has rights." Essentially all men are born equal, not that all are equally endowed with ability, but God has made all of his creatures rational and moral beings. Created in God's image every person has within him the elements of the divine and the seeds of immortality. Anything else in God's universe may be subdued by superior power but "lay not your hands on God's rational offspring!"[15]

The chief aim of civil society should be "to secure rights, not accumulate wealth." In starting with the premise that the slave is property, every defense of human rights is trodden in the dust. Slavery deprives a man of any chance to make his own decisions and seek his own happiness. Not even in self defense dare a slave repel injury from a white man. He cannot acquire property. Even

[14] Albert Barnes, *An Inquiry into the Scriptural Views of Slavery* (Philadelphia: Perkins and Purves, 1846), p. 97.

[15] William E. Channing, *Works* (Boston: James Munroe and Co., 1847), II, 17-30.

his wife and children may be torn from him when it suits his master's pleasure. To be completely at the mercy of others is to be divested of what composes the real substance of humanity, and is an iniquitous infraction of inalienable sacred rights.[16]

The anti-slavery theologians may be seen as forerunners of schools of thought on the racial question which have persevered to the present day. Following the emancipation of the slaves much of the moral fervor on the whole subject was lost by the Protestants in the North. Their energies consumed by other issues, the major Protestant denominations were strangely silent about the evils of Jim Crowism which were introduced after the reconstruction era and became firmly entrenched some decades later. Even the proponents of the Social Gospel at the turn of the century, led by men like Walter Rauschenbusch and Shailer Mathews, had little to say about racial injustice. Only during the last few decades has there been a genuine awakening among American churchmen regarding the necessity for establishing "an integrated church in an integrated society."[17]

In recent years denominational and interdenominational periodicals have been loaded with articles on the race question. Church conventions have almost without exception passed resolutions endorsing integration and lamenting racial prejudice. Among more conversative evangelicals we can see the mid-twentieth-century counterpart of Theodore Weld and his colleagues. Among the leading spokesmen for the National Council of Churches and more liberal churchmen we can trace some of the thinking of William Channing.[18]

As it was at the time of the polemics over slavery, so today the Bible continues to be searched and analyzed for favorable and un-

[16] *Ibid.*, pp. 31-50.

[17] Cf. Frank S. Loescher, *The Protestant Church and the Negro* (New York: Association Press, 1948).

[18] E.g., Liston Pope, former Dean of Yale Divinity School and author of *The Kingdom Beyond Caste;* Homer Jack, for many years Unitarian minister in Evanston, Illinois, who frequently contributes articles to the *Christian Century.*

favorable evidence. Among the anti-segregationists, as an heir of the Bible-quoting abolitionists, one might think of Everett Tilson who wrote four years after the Supreme Court decision of 1954 to demonstrate that the proof texts of anti-integrationists are not persuasive and are based on faulty assumptions. For example, to refute the argument of racial purists that separation of the races is a divine mandate, he cites instances of intermarriage between Hebrews and non-Hebrews and points out that the genealogy of Jesus included Rachab, a woman of the Canaanites. Intermarriage in the story of Ruth, and the conversion of Assyrians in the Book of Jonah, he pits against the exclusivism of Ezra and Nehemiah who compelled the Jews to give up their foreign wives during the postexilic period.[19] When one reads these retorts to segregationists, he cannot escape the impression that the arguments pro and con are essentially the same as they were in the debate over slavery.

Most non-liberals who are not segregationists prefer to think of themselves as "middle-of-the-roaders" and fit best into our third category to be considered in the next chapter. But some self-acclaimed "evangelicals" have deplored the neglect of social ethics by fundamentalists and call for meaningful involvement in the "race revolution." William Henry Anderson, Jr., a pastor of the United Presbyterian Church in Pittsburgh, is representative of this trend. "The robes of the evangelicals," he complains, "may be unstained by contact with the Negroes; but these robes show a tinge of yellow from not being cleansed and bleached by a bit of travail and blood." What can enlightened evangelicals do? With their stress on biblical authority they can assert "the oneness of all believers in Christ." Once and for all they should renounce the "misuse of Scripture" in furthering segregation. The narrative about Noah's sons "has nothing to do with race." The line of demarcation in both Testaments is between believer and unbeliever, not between races. "The presence or absence of living faith in Christ is

[19] Everett Tilson, *Segregation and the Bible* (Nashville: Abingdon, 1958), pp. 32-40.

the only biblical criterion for separation among people." Any congregation which refuses membership to a person of another race who qualifies in every other respect "does not deserve to be called a church." Evangelicals, Anderson admonishes, must cease to ally themselves with reactionary political and social forces and identify themselves with legitimate aspirations of the Negro people. Lay leaders should stand behind their pastors in supporting full integration in church and community.[20]

It is no doubt accurate to assert that the fervor of the pre-Civil War abolitionists has not been caught, at least not before 1963, by white Christians, but by intrepid Negro Christians. The speeches and writings of men like Martin Luther King are those which sound most like the crusaders against slavery. Without allowing for any extenuating circumstances or apologies for gradualism, they unhesitatingly anathematize segregation in all of its manifestations as a despicable evil. At the National Conference on Religion and Race Dr. King threw out the gauntlet to the hundreds of church leaders who had assembled together in Chicago on January 14, 1963, to commemorate the centennial of the Emancipation Proclamation:

> [Let Christians and Jews] . . . affirm that every human life is a reflex of divinity, [and] that every act of injustice mars and defaces the image of God in man. . . . Love is not emotional hash. It is not spineless sentimentality which refuses to take courageous action against evil for fear someone may be offended. . . . Will we continue to bless a status quo that needs to be blasted and reassure a social order that needs to be reformed. . . . Will we continue to march to the drum beat of conformity and respectability, or will we . . . march only to the soul-saving music of eternity?[21]

"Liberals" and "evangelicals" joined hands in most American de-

[20] William Henry Anderson, Jr., "Evangelicals and the Race Revolution," *Christianity Today,* VIII (October 25, 1963), pp. 6-8.

[21] Martin Luther King, Jr., "A Challenge to the Churches and Synagogues," in *Race: Challenge to Religion,* ed. Matthew Ahman (Chicago: Regnery, 1963), pp. 161, 164, 169.

nominations to renounce racism in the 1960's as they had renounced slavery more than a hundred years earlier. Open occupancy in housing was upheld by the American Baptist Convention in 1963. The Annual Conference of the Church of the Brethren, meeting during the same year, underscored the necessity for immediate remedial action: "*the time is now* [emphasis in the original] to understand that racial reconciliation is built only on the foundation of racial justice, that justice delayed is justice denied." Concurrently the Disciples of Christ decided to raise a special fund of no less than $300,000 to intensify and augment a program of "concern" for brotherhood. The College of Bishops of the Christian Methodist Episcopal Church explicitly commended such groups as the Southern Christian Leadership Conference and the National Urban League for their courage in seeking redress for the many injustices heaped upon Negro Americans.[22]

[22] *Interracial News Service,* January-February, 1964, National Council of the Churches of Christ in the U. S. A.

6 Theological Neutrality toward the Controversy over Slavery

Some theologians, and perhaps the bulk of ordinary Christians, during and prior to the Civil War, could not be classified as either defenders of the slavocracy or the pro-emancipation crusade. We must delineate a third position, a kind of *via media* which endeavored to mediate between the "extremists on both sides." More accurately, however, it was a stance of aloofness which relegated the issue of slavery to the political and social realm and declared that it was "not the business of the church" to interfere. Charles Hodge, the eminent systematic theologian at Princeton, rejected abolitionism on biblical grounds by asserting that slavery is not outlawed as a sin per se in the Scriptures. The strategy of abolitionism, he was convinced, was unfortunate, increasing resistance to change in the South and fomenting dissension among the friends of the Negro in the North. Together with William Paley, whose teaching he was echoing, he shared the hope that slavery might be terminated through a gradual elevation of the Negro.[1]

After raking slave-holding ministers over the coals of his inflamed anger, abolitionist Albert Barnes observes with chagrin that there are also pastors and laymen who, whatever their real sentiments are, remain silent, or by their vowed conservatism are classed

[1] John R. Bodo, *The Protestant Clergy and Public Issues, 1812-1848* (Princeton: Princeton University Press, 1954).

in the public mind with the apologists for slavery. Whereas these soft-spoken people might not sanction the brutalities of enforced servitude, neither can they be relied upon to give backing to emancipation efforts. In support of their "leave it alone" position, Barnes notes, they take refuge in biblical precepts about non-violence and the danger of agitation. Peace at any price would appear to be their motto:

> They regard that which is fixed and settled as so important that it is better that a wrong should be endured, rather than to peril the safety of existing institutions by any change whatever. They have affixed to the Union of the States such a value that it is fairly inferred from their opinion that it is better that any evil should be endured—that any number of millions of human beings should be held in hopeless bondage—than that the existence of the Union should be perilled. They have affixed an odious idea to the word abolitionist, and, so far as their influence goes led the public to do it also. . . .[2]

One need only substitute the word "agitator" for "abolitionist" in the recrimination of Barnes and he would immediately find it descriptive of a contemporary Christian posture toward the Negro revolt.

Samuel Seabury, to mention one pertinent example of what Barnes was talking about in his own generation, played the music of moderation. Following in the footsteps of our discreet fathers, Seabury pleaded, implies that we must not act rashly in trying to overthrow a system which has become deeply entrenched in some sections of America. The slave trade should be annihilated as far as possible, but domestic slavery must be tolerated "on grounds both of justice and expediency." By tolerating the lesser evil, Seabury was convinced, the nation could be preserved from dissolution. The enemies of slavery are making the mistake of elevating the individual above the state. To desire full equality for slaves and

[2] Albert Barnes, *Church and Slavery* (Philadelphia: Parry and McMillan, 1857), p. 17.

women, and to deprive the rich of their property to appease the poor, would be antithetical to "the genius of modern civilization and the law of Nature and of Christ."[3]

Seabury prefaces his writing by announcing his aim to subtract "from this vexed controversy . . . its moral, religious, and social element" so that it can be dispassionately analyzed and "disposed of on merely economical and political grounds."[4]

Seabury argues that servitude could well have been part of "the age of innocence" just as the relation between husband and wife, child and parent. Citing a passage from Augustine's *City of God* he endeavors to demonstrate that the relationship between master and slave is part of the natural order, "is productive of no hardship, and is accompanied with no disgrace, but is alike beneficial and honorable." What has brought degradation and misery into this unobjectionable arrangement of society is "the abuse of man's free will." The blight of sin has made "masters imperious and servants turbulent, and has thus caused the relation to be upheld by force." It is not the function of Christianity to abolish what God has ordained as good, but which has been perverted by the contrariness of man. The cure for the present malady is for Christians to breathe into the natural orders the "love of God and man."[5]

Seabury was prepared to compromise with the South to avert further sectional strife. Granting that the founders of the Republic were opposed to retaining slaves because they deemed it economically inefficient and politically undesirable, let it be remembered that "*their love of justice* [italicized in the original] was stronger than their aversion to slavery." Appreciation for the firm bond between slave and master deterred them from depriving the former of his security and the latter of "his right to the slave's labor." Even if some of them disapproved of enforced servitude "*their love*

[3] Samuel Seabury, *American Slavery Distinguished from the Slavery of English Theorists and Justified by the Law of Nature* (New York: Mason Brothers, 1861), pp. 312-14.

[4] *Ibid.*, p. iv. [5] *Ibid.*, pp. 91, 92.

of union" [his emphasis] induced them to "adopt a Constitution which protected slavery in States which had no intention to abolish it." After seventy years have elapsed, Seabury continues, and the settlement of another territory has become a bone of contention, it will be wise to "revere" the example of the fathers. "Let us love territory much, justice and union more."[6]

While many Episcopalians and Presbyterians in the mid-twentieth century continue to disavow the NAACP as emphatically as they do the Ku Klux Klan, and try to walk the tight rope between zealots and bigots, it should be recognized that their national assemblies have released strong pronouncements against enforced segregation and the denial of basic human rights to Negro citizens. The social perspective of a Hodge or a Seabury is no longer discernible among the vocal leaders of the present generation. In 1962 the United Presbyterian Church in the U.S.A. deplored violations of voting rights and urged renewed commitment to the goal of a nonsegregated church in a nonsegregated society. In 1963 southern Presbyterians (the Presbyterian Church in the U.S.) decried racial barriers as inconsistent with Christian convictions and encouraged churchmen to take the initiative in establishing "a relationship of mutual trust and affection" between Negroes and whites so that shameful episodes might be averted. Through its National Council the Protestant Episcopal church expressed its dismay over the troubled situation at the University of Mississippi in 1962 and called "upon its members to face seriously their obligation to conform to federal and Supreme Court orders in regard to giving all students equal access to our public schools."[7]

With few exceptions Roman Catholics were not outspoken partisans in the sectional disputes that preceded the Civil War. According to the official teaching of the church, human bondage was not morally reprehensible in itself as long as the conditions expounded

[6] *Ibid.*, pp. 310-12.

[7] Cf. *Interracial News Service*, January-February, 1964, National Council of Churches of Christ in the U. S. A.

by the theologians for a "just servitude" were kept in mind. Otherwise, the sons and daughters of the church in the United States were free to follow their own inclinations.

In the South, Roman Catholics were so much of a minority that it would have been precarious for them to have dissented from prevailing practices. "In his attitude towards the 'peculiar institution' and in the management of his slaves," Madeline Hooke Rice remarks, "the average Catholic differed not at all from his Protestant neighbor."[8]

In the North there was more diversity of opinion. No outright abolitionism was evident, but otherwise there were various gradations of sentiment. Some churchmen were critical of the slave system, and during the war took up the cudgels for emancipation. On the other side were men who contributed to the positive pro-slavery point of view. All the while, "the traditional policy of the Catholic Church . . . encouraged a certain unity of approach" which must patently be classified as part of the theological neutrality toward slavery.[9] Church members were not disciplined or excommunicated for holding slaves. Nor was slavery stamped with any "imprimatur" of unqualified approval.

Some anti-Romanists have taken a dimmer view of the papal church in its relation to slavery. Alarmed by a favorable Negro response in the 1950's to the blandishments of Roman Catholic clergy, one North Carolinian ransacked the libraries in his state to adduce incriminating evidence against them, even to the point of blaming priests for inciting the assassination of Abraham Lincoln. This writer, evincing a widespread Catholic phobia, accused the medieval church of holding people in bondage, the greedy "Catholic" monarchs of Spain and Portugal of practicing the cruelties of slavery in the New World, the French Catholics in New Orleans of

[8] Madeline Hooke Rice, *American Catholic Opinion in the Slavery Controversy* (New York: Columbia University Press, 1944), p. 152.

[9] Cf. *ibid.*, p. 156: "Throughout the course of the slavery controversy ecclesiastical leaders insisted upon the official neutrality of the Church."

abetting the slave trade, and Bishop John England of South Carolina of fostering slavery within his own diocese. "To help some of Adam's fallen race to avoid Satan's masterpieces of deception" he enumerates almost incredible instances of how the church sacrificed its principles for the sake of expediency. What he ends up with is a one-sided exaggeration of Roman Catholic complicity with the vile system, and neglects to mention that all Christendom has shared in this shameful betrayal of its Master.[10] No doubt some Catholics in the ante-bellum days could authentically be classified as proslavery, but by and large they fit more readily into the neutralist camp.

The American hierarchy was predominantly European in origin and understandably influenced by its intimate ties with that continent. In the Old World, the church was on the defensive against liberalism, Marxism, anti-clericalism, and secularism. The leaders of American reform movements were likely to be treated with suspicion because they were linked in the Catholic mind with the dreaded "revolutionaries" and "Red Republicans" of Europe. The fact that many of the active abolitionists were Protestants added to the distrust of Roman Catholics. Generally there was a spirit of conservatism towards domestic problems, particularly among the clergy. Irish-Americans were obsessed with their own persecution at the hands of England and could not become excited over British or Anglo-American emancipation societies. The involvement of rationalist and freethinking émigrés in abolitionist agitation was enough to alienate German Catholics. The affiliation of the Roman Catholic citizenry with the Democratic party was another factor which dissuaded them from favoring immediate liberation and caused them to oppose federal interference with the rights supposedly reserved for the states. In addition to all this, the prospect of emancipation alarmed Catholic laborers who viewed the Negroes with antagonism as future competitors for jobs.

[10] Cf. Richard Roscoe Miller, *Slavery and Catholicism* (Durham, N. C.: North State Publishers, 1957). The quotation may be found in the preface.

Editorials written in papers like the *Metropolitan Record* and the Baltimore *Mirror* were negative toward the goal of emancipation. Councils and synods during this tense period cautiously followed a policy of confining their deliberations to the "morals and discipline of the Church." Roman Catholic soldiers fought on both sides in the fratricide which bled the nation. There was no serious sectional rupture over the slavery issue despite a certain amount of polemical correspondence between northern and southern ecclesiastics.[11]

By 1860 it could be said that an unofficial "Catholic position" subscribed to by the majority of the laity had crystalized:

> It rested first upon the theological argument which denied that slavery was intrinsically wrong. It recognized the existence of evils in the slave system which made eventual emancipation desirable, but it held that such emancipation should come gradually and with due regard for the welfare of society and the protection of the property rights of the owners. Finally, it condemned abolitionism absolutely, both for its methods and for its associations.[12]

In the last few decades the Roman communion in the United States has moved away from compromise and neutrality to profess a deeper sympathy with the Negro cause. On Pentecost Sunday in 1934 white and colored Catholic laymen came together in New York City and launched a concerted program for interracial justice. By 1951 a group of southern collegians adopted a declaration affirming: "We must accept the fact that the doctrine of the Mystical Body applies here and now in the South." In 1954 the Catholic Bishops of the United States prepared a statement explicitly renouncing "compulsory segregation" and endorsing equal opportunities for Negroes.[13] Catholic schools in St. Louis were desegregated

[11] Cf. Rice, *op. cit.,* pp. 153, 154, 156, 158. [12] *Ibid.,* p. 155.

[13] Cf. John LaFarge, *The Catholic Viewpoint on Race Relations* (Garden City, N. Y.: Hannover House, 1960), pp. 68, 70, 186-92.

by ecclesiastical edict, despite tenacious lay resistance, long before the public schools took similar action. In New Orleans recalcitrant racists were excommunicated when they refused to abstain from turbulent school riots.

Roman Catholic repudiation of the neutralist posture became official when the American Bishops agreed (with Cardinal McIntyre of Los Angeles, a lone dissenter) that inequities grounded on race require rectification because they are moral issues, not merely political problems. This position was reaffirmed in 1963 just prior to the march on Washington.

Pastoral letters calling for the integration of Roman Catholic schools have been promulgated in a number of sensitive areas as Atlanta, Georgia, New Orleans, Louisiana, and elsewhere. Even intransigent Mississippians were confronted with the unwelcome announcement that beginning September, 1964, Catholic pupils would be admitted to first grade "without regard to race."[14] This step marked the first breakthrough in the ironclad system of segregation which had prevailed in the elementary schools of Mississippi.

Catholic scholastic philosophy has maintained that the conscience is the ultimate judge of action. According to this approach, the task of the priests is to form and inform the conscience of their parishioners. Obviously this allows maximum latitude in interpretation and application. Some Catholics can remain neutralists believing that the church should say and do little or nothing to influence social change. Others can become ardent advocates of integration. And more than a few can defend forms of segregation which they claim do not offend their consciences. Baffled by this apparent confusion a retired Archbishop, T. D. Roberts, S. J. (Bombay, India) was convinced that it would be vital for the Second Vatican Council to ponder and reformulate the role of conscience in the moral response of the individual to the church's teaching. If

[14] A pastoral letter was prepared by Bishop Gerow of the Natchez-Jackson diocese. Cf. *Chronicle* (San Francisco), August 10, 1964.

"conscience is the manifestation of natural law" it should not lead to contradictory results.[15]

Even by the 1960's not all Roman Catholics had retreated from the "neutralist" stance. Nothwithstanding Pope John XXIII's affirmation of social justice in his encyclical *Pacem Terris,* and pro-integration sentiment among clergy and laity in some dioceses, ecclesiastical silence and inaction have been preserved in such an area as southern California where militant anti-communist organizations like the Cardinal Mindszenty Foundation thrive. Cardinal McIntyre, disregarding Negro Catholic protests and appeals from his own priests, has steadfastly refused to treat racial discrimination as a burden on the Christian conscience. In full accord with the traditional pre-Civil War theology of the Roman church he has reiterated the familiar distinction between "political issues" and "moral issues" and admonished his parish priests to desist from preaching on the racial question. In the summer of 1964, Father DuBay, who was ministering to a Negro parish in Los Angeles, became so perturbed over the Archbishop's "neutralism" that he cabled the Pope with a plea for his superior's removal from office for "gross malfeasance" and "abuses of authority" and for conducting "a vicious program of intimidation and repression" against clergymen and laymen who tried to respond constructively to the Negro revolt. The impetuous young priest was compelled to capitulate, but his bold action cast the spotlight of publicity on a populous sector of the Roman Catholic church which has been reluctant to agree that Christian theology demands the full emancipation of the Negro and open support for civil rights.

That what is officially proclaimed as "neutrality" ("you can't legislate morality"; "wherever law and local custom permitted, the Church has practiced integration in its churches, schools, and social service department") is nearly always a facade for concealing prejudice was again exemplified by the private comments attributed to

[15] Telephone conversation August 12, 1964, with A. V. Krebs, Jr., Roman Catholic free-lance writer.

Cardinal McIntyre: "After all, white parents have a right to defend their daughters. . . . To advocate black nuns in white schools and white nuns in black schools [is an insult]." In an atmosphere where rights wing extremists including the John Birch Society wield enormous influence, doing nothing to aid the Negro cause has, in practice, meant an almost total neglect of social responsibility.[16]

Not too dissimilar from the Roman Catholic position sketched in the preceding paragraphs was the approach of the Lutherans, especially the confessionally orthodox groups who immigrated to the United States from Germany during the period of the most intense theological controversy over slavery.

Among the "native" Lutherans who were mostly settled along the Atlantic seaboard there were some vigorous disagreements with tempers flaring up on both sides of the Mason-Dixon line. The German settlers in Pennsylvania and elsewhere were usually opposed to slave ownership in which only 3.7 percent of the whole German nationality in the United States were involved. However, it was the regular policy of the Lutheran church not to be concerned with social problems which had political implications. From 1790 to 1838 there are no records to indicate that any Lutheran Synod in its general or district conventions took any action favorable or unfavorable on the slavery question.[17] Where Negroes were held in bondage by Lutherans they usually received baptism and Christian instruction. In North Carolina, Lutheran parishes were not free of abolitionist sentiment, and three of the six anti-slavery leaders in that southern state were of German ancestry.[18] Eventually, when the Civil War broke out, the Lutherans in the South withdrew from the General Synod to organize an independent body. For the most part, though, even these more Americanized Lutherans

[16] A full account of the DuBay case and Catholicism in Los Angeles may be found in *The Commonweal* (July 10, 1964).

[17] Cf. Charles William Heathcote, *The Lutheran Church and the Civil War* (Burlington, Iowa: Lutheran Literary Board, 1919), pp. 43, 44.

[18] Cf. William Henry Gehrke, "Negro Slavery among the Germans in North Carolina," *North Carolina Historical Review,* XIV (October, 1937), p. 320.

"in the Muhlenberg tradition"[19] tended to preserve a policy of neutrality toward slavery.

One of the most widely distributed and influential journals, the *Lutheran Observer,* under the ownership and editorship of the Reverend Benjamin Kurtz, was quite representative of the kind of thinking that predominated among Lutheran ecclesiastics. The ill-fated attempt to resettle liberated Negroes in the American-created Republic of Liberia was consistently supported. Lutheran caution and aversion to strife made the editor skeptical about the abolitionist movement. Without impugning the sincerity of their motives he dismissed their scheme as an absurdity. The extreme agitation of the Anti-Slavery Society, he feared, might cause the dissolution of the Union and might lead to a torrent of bloodshed. Well intentioned as the abolitionists may be "they are most seriously injuring the cause of the colored people in this country, and will be found at last to have been among their worst and most dangerous enemies." In the issue of August 21, 1835, Kurtz disapproves of the action of fifty students at Phillip's Academy, Andover, who withdrew from the school because their principal refused to grant them permission to form an Anti-Slavery Society. The principal is praised for "the judicious and manly stand he has taken."[20]

As the anti-slavery crusade gathered momentum the moderate position of the editor of the *Lutheran Observer* drew the fire of some incensed and irate readers. Impervious to these complaints the editor doggedly refused to change his neutralist attitude that suggested it would be imprudent to open the pages of his periodical to either the "sublime merits of slavery" or "the idle fancies of immediate abolitionists." The newly founded Franckean Synod

[19] The towering figure in eighteenth-century American Lutheranism had been Henry Melchior Muhlenberg, a pietist trained at the University of Halle. His memorable achievements included rallying the scattered Lutherans in the colonies, encouraging the training of native clergy, and leading in the organization of the Ministerium of Pennsylvania in 1748.

[20] Robert Fortenaugh, "The Representative Lutheran Periodical Press and Slavery, 1831-1860," *The Lutheran Church Quarterly,* VIII (April, 1935) pp. 151-53.

(Lutheran) which unanimously passed four resolutions against slavery was looked upon with suspicion. The cruelties of the slave trade were denounced. The chivalry of the South which had been satisfied with his "hands off" policy merited words of appreciation. The action of some Lutherans in circulating the uncompromising abolition paper, the *New York Evangelist,* written by ultra-new school Presbyterians who have often expressed anti-Lutheran sentiments, caused him to wrinkle his editorial brow. In the issue of April 12, 1844, notice is taken of the report that William Lloyd Garrison was campaigning for the elimination of capital punishment. Here is more evidence of the dangerous character of these rabid agitators. What mischief will they be concocting next?[21]

Although the Fugitive Slave Law may be too stringent, the editor admonished his readers to realize that it is constitutional and must be obeyed. In accord with the Lutheran tradition secular authority must be respected. No one is exempted because the government makes mistakes or establishes regulations of which we do not approve.[22]

Even Lutherans, however, no matter how much indoctrinated in the virtues of passivity and acquiescence to the status quo, could not entirely evade the tempest which surrounded them. A minister from Georgia wrote in 1854 that he was conducting successful revivals which included Negroes. Gratuitously he added the remark that the colored population in the South is "far better off than thousands who live in a land of so-called freedom." Each person ought to be content with the station in which Providence has placed him, and southerners knew where to place the Negro. This sectional bias elicited the retort from a northern minister writing in the *Lutheran Observer:* Would the Georgia cleric be content if he were a slave? Should not the Good Samaritan be reprimanded for interfering with the existing situation as he found it? Does the brother ever think of the "poor slaves" when he preaches on this

[21] *Ibid.*, pp. 154-57.
[22] *Ibid.*, pp. 159-60.

familiar text? Meanwhile the conciliatory-minded editor was finding it increasingly difficult to placate the antagonists. He regrets that he permitted even this much controversy to upset the equilibrium of his periodical.[23]

In 1856, when the cautious Mr. Kurtz so much as dared to intimate that Brooks was not justified in browbeating Sumner in the celebrated Senate scandal, he was greeted with vicious letters from the South vilifying his character and threatening his life. Belatedly the hitherto noncommital editor realized that fanaticism in the South could more than equal the vehemence of any Yankee abolitionist propaganda. Southern readers threatened to cancel their subscriptions and looked forward to the establishment of an independent Lutheran journal in the South in which they would be free to express their own sentiments.[24]

In another publication, *The Missionary,* a front page contribution to the issue of December 10, 1857, by a theologian by the name of Bachman, expressed a tolerant view toward slaveholding. In his opinion the detractors of slavery were ill-informed. The treatment of the African is generally kind and humane. After recognizing his natural inferiority, it would only be detrimental to the welfare of the Negro to grant him freedom, and thereby sentence him to a worse fate. The paternal concern and generosity displayed by the southern masters are to be extolled. The Bible not only permits slavery; in some instances it enjoins the practice. When some incendiaries deplore the evils of slavery from the pulpit they are to be faulted for mingling politics and religion. "It is well to remember Luther's counsel of obedience to the laws of the land. . . ."

The editor of *The Missionary,* Dr. Passavant, did not concur with these judgments and replied in an editorial entitled "Freedom Bet-

[23] *Ibid.,* pp. 160, 161.

[24] *Ibid.,* p. 162. During the Civil War southern Lutherans created a schism by seceding from the General Synod and organizing the United Synod of the South. The breach was not healed until the reunion of 1918.

ter than Bondage" in which he contended for the righteousness and practicality of emancipation, and concluded with this prophetic estimate of the Negroes: "The day of their pupilage is past, and they deserve to go forth as men and brethren, in the full and virtuous enjoyment of life, liberty, and the pursuit of happiness."[25]

More detached from the mainstream of American life, and more immersed in the Lutheran orthodoxy of the seventeenth century, were the mid-western Lutherans of German extraction. Led by Saxon immigrants in reaction against rationalism in the mother country "the German Evangelical Lutheran Synod of Missouri, Ohio, and Other States" was organized in 1847 at Chicago. With an emphasis on pure religion they entered into doctrinal controversies with more liberal-minded Lutherans and sought to safeguard their members from all corroding influences such as humanism and atheism. Led by C. F. W. Walther, the "Lutheran Pope of the West,"[26] they entered the fray against all anti-Christian forces of the day. As the first president of the Synod and as director of its theological seminary Walther was preeminent in the councils of the new church body. Unalterably opposed to the radicalism which he had left behind in Germany he used pen and pulpit to help send it scurrying for cover wherever it reared its head in the land of his adoption. The basic error which he detected in the philosophy of all the political and religious liberals was the assumption that freedom and equality constituted the highest good, and that man was capable of attaining this highest good by developing his own innate potentialities. That man might be the master of his own destiny was a blasphemous thought to one who was reared to believe in natural depravity and justification by God's grace alone. The claim that all men were free and equal because Christ died to liberate them was to Walther and his associates a serious misunderstanding of Scripture. Spiritual freedom was not to be identified with temporal free-

[25] *Ibid.*, pp. 166-70.

[26] The phrase is that of C. F. Wittke in *We Who Built America: The Saga of the Immigrant* (New York: Prentice-Hall, 1939), p. 225.

dom. Spiritual freedom could be preserved within the framework of a servant-master relationship. Where slavery existed it should not be uprooted by rebellion. Obedience is an integral part of God's law.[27]

A sharp distinction was made between the temporal and spiritual aspects of life. By birth a man was a citizen of an earthly kingdom. By virtue of his faith in Christ he was at the same time a member of the heavenly kingdom. These two realms are not to be confused. Church and state must be kept separate. Religion and politics must not be intermingled. Questions concerning secession, slavery, and political parties should not occupy the attention of congregational meetings or church conferences.[28]

No resolutions or pronouncements on slavery appear in the reports of the conventions of the Missouri Synod before 1860. But early in 1863 a series of articles on slavery were submitted to the official denominational periodical *Der Lutheraner* by William Sihler, a close collaborator with Dr. Walther. In a footnote appended to the first installment he was careful to stress that he is not treating the political aspects of slavery, as though one could readily subdivide the burning issue into its "spiritual" and "social" components.[29]

The bulk of Sihler's writings was concerned with expounding two main points. First, slaveholding cannot be denounced in the name of Christianity because it is not contrary to the teaching of God's word. Slavery is a consequence and punishment for sin, but not sinful in itself. Secondly, slaves and their masters alike stand under the wrath of God and must be rescued from their common plight by being freed from their sins through faith in the saving power of Christ's sacrificial death. Outside of these considerations slavery

[27] Cf. *Lehre und Wehre,* IX (January, 1863), p. 5.

[28] Paul M. Kavasch, "The Lutheran Church—Missouri Synod During the Early Years of the Civil War," *Concordia Historical Institute Quarterly,* XXXI (October, 1958), pp. 68-74.

[29] *Der Lutheraner,* XIX (February 1, 1863), p. 89. (All translations from the original German are the responsibility of the present writer.)

is primarily a political problem outside the province of the church's responsibility.[30]

Sihler considers it shameful that men pretending to be ministers of the gospel have become abolitionist speechmakers and agitators. When they offer succor to fugitive slaves they are flagrantly violating the law. The revolutionary conspiracies, and the emancipation fervor they have whipped up, have had as their end result the miseries of the Civil War. The abolitionists are to be classified with the *Schwaermer* (fanatics). The inflammatory utterances of William Lloyd Garrison frightened the Lutherans who visualized a reincarnation of Thomas Muentzer and dreaded a repetition of anything comparable to the Peasant's Revolt which was such a severe setback to the cause of the Reformation in the sixteenth century. There was a marked tendency among the American Lutherans, including Walther and Sihler, to warn against any interference with the established order. Almost any kind of tyranny would be preferable to the chaos and destruction that accompany insurrection. If and when slavery disappears, the Christian must conform to the new situation. But it is a diabolical distortion of the New Testament proclamation of freedom in Christ to use it as a trumpet call for revolutionary social change.

The American Lutheran theologians of this period were uncreative and unimaginative on a subject like slavery because they seem to have had their thinking stifled within the narrow framework of a static society. Procedures and customs which may have been feasible in the days of Abraham were transposed from a middle eastern pastoral setting to the United States at a time when the country was becoming industrialized. The machine age was dawning and the repercussions were little understood. Unwarranted generalizations and laws universally binding for all time were made out of pastoral counsel which St. Paul intended to meet particular immediate social needs.

[30] *Ibid.*, XIX (March 15, 1863), pp. 113-15.

Sihler formulates an expedient explanation of why Africans were brought to the United States. In this country they are really faring better than if they had remained in their native habitat where they might have been captured as slaves of war and become victims of human sacrifices made to false gods. By being transported to America they have escaped an environment cursed with superstitions and bondage to the devil.[31]

Dr. Sihler reflected his European Lutheran background when he wrote about the duties of slaveholders toward their slaves. All are brethren in Christ. In a broad sense the slaves should be regarded as members of the household. As among the Old Testament patriarchs and with the landed aristocracy on their estates in semi-feudal Germany, the planters should exercise paternal benevolence and provide for all the physical requirements of their slaves.[32]

Reporting on the impressions of a German sea officer who had visited the Negro Republic in Africa, Sihler took a dim view of the resettlement project. As an immigrant theologian trained in a German university he was inclined to compare the Negro agricultural workers with German peasants and found the former deficient in ambition and assiduity. Natural resources are abundant, but the will to progress and erect a civilization [according to Western standards?] is lacking. Wisely enough, however, Sihler declines to pass an unconditional judgment on the incapability of the Negro race to absorb the "superior" culture of the whites. The eventual disposition of the whole slavery problem and the future destiny of the Negro people in America he committed into the hands of God who alone knows the real potential of his creatures.[33]

While professing theological neutrality Dr. C. F. W. Walther displayed a partisan attitude in favor of the South during the Civil War. Quite understandably his personal views were rather embarrassing to the main constituency of his denomination which was cen-

[31] *Ibid.* (February 1, 1863), pp. 90, 91.
[32] *Ibid.* (March 15, 1863), pp. 113-15.
[33] *Ibid.* (March 15, 1863), p. 39.

tered in northern states like Illinois and Wisconsin. Most Germans disagreed with the Lutheran theologian and are credited with helping to keep Missouri out of the confederacy. Fraternal relations with the Norwegian Synod were strained when students came North with disquieting reports about secessionist sentiment on the St. Louis faculty. When the Norwegian professor at Concordia Seminary failed to deny the rumors there was clamor for a break with "Missouri."[34]

The inglorious aftermath of this kind of thinking which refused to denounce slavery in principle as a moral evil was still discernible as late as 1935 when President H. A. Klein of the Lutheran seminary in Springfield, Illinois, stamped his "imprimatur" on a book by Anna Hoppe defending the slavery system as she remembered it from frequent contacts with former slaveholders and their descendants: "What she says is not fiction . . . or ideal representation of conditions, but rather a collection of historical facts which cannot be denied."[35]

Miss Hoppe, subjective in her judgments and with a dubious arrangement of historical data, manages to exonerate the South of any odium connected with slavery. The villainous British who indulged in the slave traffic maneuvered the innocent southerners into the uncomfortable position where they were obliged to retain their slaves out of humanitarian motives. In any event, the slaves gained by the exchange; their comforts in America being preferable to the conditions under which they lived in Africa.[36]

An admirer of the ante-bellum South, Miss Hoppe evidently had not advanced beyond the scientific understanding of that epoch and region. With dogmatic assurance she imparts to her readers the sad fact that "Niggers" are hopelessly inferior, both in "disposition and lack of intellect." To retain the respect of a Negro you must always

[34] Cf. J. Magnus Rohne, *Norwegian American Lutheranism up to 1872* (New York: Macmillan, 1926), pp. 198, 202-04.

[35] Anna Hoppe, *Negro Slavery* (St. Louis: Rudolph Volkening Publisher, 1935), foreword.

[36] *Ibid.*, pp. 24-27.

avoid placing yourself on the same level with him. Negroes are not fit for self-government. For their own benefit, they must be controlled by others. In slaveholding days flogging was unavoidable if lazy Negroes were to be disciplined. Their natural odor is repellent. The worst evil imaginable would be miscegenation. Mulatto children are ugly. "The offspring of Whites and Negroes are never without a bodily vice." A woman who prided herself on her superior intelligence, Miss Hoppe apparently was altogether unfamiliar with the modern science of genetics: "Even an Octoroon, when married to a white man, may give birth to a coal black baby."[37]

After completing her prejudiced, unscientific portrayal of the Negro in America, Miss Hoppe emphasized that the object of her "essay" was to vindicate "the honor of countless, innocently accused slave owners, who have now passed away," and thus discharge her duty in fulfilling the commandment, "Thou shalt not bear false witness against thy neighbor."[38]

Thus under the cloak of theological neutrality, some extremely biased accounts of the slavery issue have been disseminated. Among northerners, as well as southerners, the deep-seated prejudices and irrational superstitions evoked by the presence of African slaves on our soil, have been slow in dying. They persist today to an alarming degree, even among the "educated" and those who profess Christian principles.

Theological neutrality toward political and social issues has continued to be the position of many conservative-minded Christians in America.[39] The slavery controversy has been superseded by the "race question," but the underlying arguments are similar. The functions of church and state are to be kept separate. All laws in-

[37] *Ibid.*, pp. 54-57.

[38] *Ibid.*, p. 65.

[39] This is the editorial policy of one of the most widely distributed religious journals, *Christianity Today*. "Moral issues" such as the liquor traffic call for a clearcut stand. Editorials on segregation are cautious and tend to treat it as a social problem.

volving racial segregation are to be obeyed conscientiously whether we deem them wise or not, just as Christians prior to the Civil War were obliged to permit slavery and surrender fugitive slaves when it was in accord with the law of the land. In "the visible church" the social status of the individual remains unchanged even after conversion. Some "neutralists" even argued that a special curse rests on certain races, which we cannot annul. Whether or not racial segregation is practiced is an *adiaphoron* (as was slavery), a matter undecided by the word of God and morally inconsequential.[40]

Within the last twenty years, however, there has been a marked change in some Lutheran circles. In 1941 the Reverend Andrew Schulze, who had spent a lifetime working with "Negro Missions," wrote a controversial book entitled *My Neighbor of Another Color* in which he challenged the prevalent attitudes and pleaded for a reconsideration of the rights and privileges of the Negro in church and society. Some of the inherited prejudices from slaveholding days are frankly exposed and demonstrated to be irrational such as the curse of Canaan and racial inferiority.[41]

Conservative Lutherans have begun to experience a social awakening. The *Lutheran Witness,* official publication of the Missouri Synod, editorialized on September 3, 1963: "Since integration is morally right, it is morally wrong for a Christian to oppose it or refuse to promote it on social or economic grounds."

But there are still many "unreconstructed" neutralists in Lutheran congregations and Lutheran pulpits. Champion of orthodoxy Herman Otten, was one who vigorously objected to the new tone in the *Lutheran Witness:*

> The integration issue is not a moral question at all. It is a practical matter. During the Civil War the slavery question was hotly debated

[40] Cf. essay by the Reverend Gerhard Huebener, "Scriptural Principles Concerning the Race Problem Controversy," published by *The Confessional Lutheran* (Morrison, Ill., n.d.).

[41] Andrew Schulze, *My Neighbor of Another Color* (Minneapolis: Augsburg, 1941), cf. pp. 45-52; 117-20.

> as though it were a moral issue. . . . The Missouri Synod rejected such an approach. . . . The only valid consideration was, they said, whether slavery is beneficial for the country and its people or not, and this is not a question for the Church to argue. . . . Segregation is not commanded by God. . . . Segregation is not forbidden by God. . . . Whether people are integrated or segregated, the Church's obligation remains the same to preach the Gospel to every creature.[42]

Here in capsule form we find a neat summary of "theological neutrality toward slavery" and segregation—a position which is being abandoned by many thoughtful people but which is stubbornly retained by those who need to rationalize their lack of a social conscience.

In recent years The Lutheran Human Relations Association of America has been actively promoting better racial understanding. Their publication *The Vanguard* calls for unrestricted integration and the elimination of every trace of discrimination in a way which rivals or surpasses the most advanced thinking among "liberal" Christians.[43] In 1956 The Lutheran Church—Missouri Synod, the church body founded and nurtured by the German Lutheran theologians, Walther and Sihler, passed a resolution on race relations climaxed by the statement:

> We acknowledge our responsibility as a Church to provide guidance for our members to work in the capacity of Christian citizens for the elimination of discrimination, wherever it may exist, in community, city, state, nation, and world.[44]

Three years later the same synod stressed the unity of creation and the universality of redemption as the theological basis for the "eradication of such racial or ethnic antipathies as may still persist

[42] *Lutheran News,* I (September 23, 1963), p. 2.

[43] Cp. Ralph L. Moellering, "Toward an Enlightened Christian Social Conscience," *Proceedings,* Lutheran Human Relations Institute (Valparaiso, Ind., 1956).

[44] "Proceedings of the Forty-third Regular Convention of the Lutheran Church—Missouri Synod, St. Paul, Minnesota, June 20-29, 1956," p. 459.

in our midst." In 1962 far-reaching resolutions were passed by the denomination's national convention including a provision that "sociological changes" be studied and anticipated "well in advance, so that preventive measures can be instituted to avoid unnecessary deterioration or collapse." Greater financial support and a "redistribution of leadership potential" for the benefit of inner-city churches were strongly urged. Simultaneously "the worthy aspirations of minority groups" in combating social evils were upheld.[45]

Ever since World War II a slow but perceptible rise in social consciousness throughout most of American Lutheranism has caused the major bodies to repudiate their traditional "hands off" policy. As early as 1948 the Augustana Evangelical Lutheran Church (Swedish origin) expressed opposition to racial discrimination. The United Lutheran Church in America (which had absorbed the line of descent from Benjamin Kurtz) issued a statement in 1952 which urged equality of treatment for all citizens. The Lutheran Church in America (a 1962 merger of the United Lutheran Church, the Augustana Synod, and two smaller bodies of Danish and Finnish Americans) spoke out vigorously in behalf of racial justice through its executive council in 1963.[46]

Most forthright and specific were the "fresh resolutions" adopted by the second biennial convention of the Lutheran Church in America in 1964. Institutions and agencies within the denomination were exhorted to set a pattern of racial inclusiveness in their own business involvements and employment practices. In calling pastors and acquiring staff, congregations were admonished not to "make the race of the candidate a qualification for consideration." More than ever before members were summoned to participate in positive social action designed to assure the implementation of the civil rights legislation passed by Congress. Peaceful public demon-

[45] *Human Relations: Resolutions of the Lutheran Church—Missouri Synod,* published and distributed in cooperation with the Lutheran Human Relations Association of America, 1964.

[46] Excerpts from the actions taken by constituent Synods are included in *Social Ministry* (Study Report Number 2, September, 1963), Board of Social Ministry, Lutheran Church in America, 231 Madison Avenue, New York.

strations conducted to dramatize persisting injustices were sanctioned. And in a distinct departure from Lutheran tradition, even civil disobedience was deemed permissible "if and when the means of legal recourse have been exhausted or are demonstrably inadequate."[47]

By the mid-sixties it had become evident that no matter how much complacency disguised as moderation might persist among rank and file Roman Catholics, Presbyterians, Episcopalians, and Lutherans, their leadership had largely shifted from the "neutralist" to the "abolitionist" camp.

[47] Statement on Race Relations adopted by the Second Biennial Convention of the Lutheran Church in America, Pittsburgh, Pa., July 2-9, 1964.

7 The Record and Reputation of the Church in Race Relations

For many years already it has become a hackneyed saying that the most segregated hour of the week is eleven o'clock on Sunday morning. Scores of pious resolutions passed by church conventions and increasing instances of token integration have not belied this accusation. The continuing division along racial lines is so contrary to the doctrines of the church which speak about "one Lord, one faith, one baptism, one God and Father of us all," that it has provided abundant ammunition for the attacks of cynics who deride the church's claims as phony and dismiss her pretensions as hypocrisy.

Without fear of rebuttal it can be said that the record of the Christian church in its reaction to slavery and racial injustice is utterly deplorable. Throughout history, human servitude has been either tolerated, sanctioned, or blessed by ecclesiastical leaders. Within the United States the over-all pattern, with a few notable exceptions,[1] has been to follow a policy of expediency and to conform to the prevailing climate of opinion, varying only according to the epoch or the geographical region in which the church has spoken. In the ante-bellum Cotton Kingdom this meant a fully developed theological rationalization of slavery as a "positive good."

[1] E.g., the Quaker John Woolman in colonial times, or some of the uncompromising Christian abolitionists before the Civil War.

In the Deep South today it means, at its best, preserving a discreet silence; and, at its worst, clergymen serving as chaplains for White Citizens Councils or preaching sermons on "God, the Original Segregationist."[2] In the post-Civil War North it meant the abandonment of the Negro's cause. For the American churches, with their emphasis on personal conversion and revivalism, it has led to the cultivation of an inward piety which is insensitive to social problems. Throughout our country today the admonition is still heard that preachers must keep politics out of the pulpit. By default, American Christianity has failed to perform its prophetic task and counteract the forces of evil because it has been deemed unwise or improper to touch on such "controversial issues" as desegregation in churches, schools, housing, and employment. Despite the fact that nearly all major denominations have now declared themselves in favor of integration, there has been little actual desegregation in the Protestant churches, and there is little evidence that these much-heralded pronouncements of official bodies have been taken seriously on the local level.[3]

No wonder that "kneel-ins" became part of the Negro strategy in breaking down barriers in the South! At the end of 1963 predictions were heard that demonstrations would concentrate on the churches if civil rights legislation were blocked in Congress. When demonstrations were at their height in 1960 against dime stores whose outlets in southern states refused to serve Negro customers at lunch counters, a professor of Oriental languages at the Univer-

[2] Carey Daniel, pastor of the First Baptist Church of West Dallas, Texas, and Vice-Chairman of the Dallas Chapter, Texas Citizens' Council, 1955. Cf. *supra* chap. IV, p. 63.

[3] Cf. Howard Whitman, "The Shame of Sunday Morning," *Redbook* (August, 1953), who quotes from a survey of three denominations embracing 13,597 churches in which only eight percent had members from any minority group. "As for the Negroes themselves, it is estimated that less than one percent find themselves in churches where they worship side by side with their white brothers." Cf. Ralph Lord Roy, "Church Race Policies Compared," *Christian Century* (May 30, 1956), in which he discusses the reasons why the rate of integration is slower among Protestants than with Roman Catholics; e.g., more Negro Protestants, sectarianism, diversity in forms of worship, and a democratic as opposed to an authoritarian form of church government.

sity of California in Berkeley addressed a letter to the campus newspaper, proposing that the picketing be diverted to a different target:

> If Kress and Woolworth segregate in the South and do not here, they are . . . doing what comes naturally. They have in each area determined what is—or was—likely to bring maximum patronage and profits. . . .
>
> The churches, however, maintain that they carry with them a certain other-worldliness, a certain sanctity, a yen for martyrdom even. Why haven't students seen into the inconsistency of treating chainstore owners as saints and church leaders as businessmen who can reap segregated souls in one area and integrated souls in another without conflict of conscience or parade of pickets? . . .
>
> If charity begins at home, let it begin there. Picket every church in the land until every clergyman stopped fulminating against others when those same evils are officially condoned by his own organization. To avoid rowdiness and unfairness I would suggest that members of each church picket their own edifice. If students and others have the courage to do that, then when the nationwide job of integrating the churches is accomplished I should join the picket line in front of the holdout stores. If I am any judge of human or ecclesiastical nature, I would say that the stores, individual and chain, will have integrated everywhere long before the churches have half succeeded. The armed forces were first to achieve what the spiritual forces deem unwise, inexpedient, and infeasible. If I were a student I would feel shamefaced as a picket in front of Kress when my church maintained a segregated Christ.[4]

This is a stinging indictment against the church. But who dares to say that it is undeserved? Repeated instances of compromise and indecision confront us on all sides. Ministers have appeared to lend an air of sanctity to the strategy sessions of the advocates of Caucasian supremacy and the theories of racists who promulgate the myth of innate Negro inferiority. Prayer meetings have

[4] Ralph L. Moellering, "Is the Church Retarding Integration?" *American Lutheran,* XVIII (June, 1960), p. 7.

been conducted to implore God to frustrate the "evil designs" of "Communist agitators" who would cause the races to intermingle. Church buildings are being used in the South to teach all-white classes and circumvent the Supreme Court decision of 1954.

Kyle Haselden, native southerner and associate editor of the *Christian Century,* contends that "long before the little signs—'White Only' and 'Colored'—appeared in the public utilities they had appeared in the Church."[5] It is historically inaccurate to presume that Negro Christians have been isolated in their own congregations and denominations because they preferred this arrangemen. W. D. Weatherford, in his book on *American Churches and the Negro,* cites numerous instances in which whites and Negroes worshiped together in churches before the Civil War. As long as the master-slave relationship was upheld there was little fear of physical and social contacts between Negroes and whites. Immediately following emancipation, however, with the prospect of Negroes claiming freedom and equality, the attitude changed sharply. C. Vann Woodward speaks of "the voluntary withdrawal of the Negroes"[6] at the end of the Reconstruction debacle. But actually the formation of separate Negro denominations was due to the humiliating treatment with which they were greeted in white churches. In 1795 the African Methodist Episcopal Zion Church was organized by a former slave for the specific purpose of avoiding "numerous and increasing embarrassments on account of race within the white churches." Even if it is a reminder of the unsuppressable power of the gospel and the unassailable faith of the Negro, "the Negro church stands as a symbol of the white Christian's shame."[7]

"Of all the groups devoted to social uplift," wrote W. E. B. Dubois in 1925, "I have least hope in the white Christian ministers."[8]

[5] Kyle Haselden, *The Racial Problem in Christian Perspective* (New York: Harper, 1959), p. 29.

[6] Vann Woodward, *The Strange Career of Jim Crow* (New York: Oxford University Press, 1957), p. 15.

[7] Haselden, *op. cit.,* pp. 30, 31.

[8] *Christian Century* (April 16, 1925), p. 507.

Segregation in the churches is such an irrefutable fact that this unfavorable opinion has been substantiated by almost all scholarly investigators and commentators on the subject. Reinhold Niebuhr has long ago labelled the failure to cope with the race issue American Protestantism's most glaring weakness. Gunnar Myrdal, in his exhaustive study of the Negro problem in America, wrote:

> The observer feels that the very incompatibility between the uncompromising Christian creed, on the one hand, and the actual caste relations, on the other, is a reason why white ministers in the South keep so aloof from the race problem and why the white church in the South has generally played so inconsequential a part in changing race relations.[9]

The Marxist contention has been that religion is the opium of the people. Accordingly the Communist tirade has charged repeatedly that Christian teachings are used to "throw dust in the eyes" of the toiling masses and distract them from temporal goals to a "pie in the sky" reward hereafter. Kyle Haselden depicts the church as the "purveyor of arrant sedatives" in its use of religion to pacify and subdue the Negro. For documentation of this serious accusation he quotes from an address delivered by Charles Cotesworth Pinckney before the Agricultural Society of South Carolina on August 18, 1829. On that date, which Haselden says "marked the beginning of a vigorous campaign for the evangelizing of the Negro," Pinckney proposed to his aristocratic peers that they provide religious instruction for their slaves for two reasons, both beneficial to the planters. First, he observed, such an effort to convert the Negroes would placate the consciences of sensitive southerners who were upset by the insinuation of the abolitionists that slaveholding was immoral and incongruous with membership in the Christian church. Second, Pinckney suggested that the inculcation of Christianity in the Negro "would tend to make a more

[9] Gunnar Myrdal, *An American Dilemma* (New York: Harper, 1948), II, 868.

docile, obedient, and tractable slave, adding moral suasion to statute and the lash. . . ."[10] The same approach, we know, is being used in South Africa today where the State Information Office in Pretoria complained that the Bantus were resisting apartheid. This government office suggested that perhaps Christian education could overcome their opposition and released the statement: "Good mission policy is good Government policy in South Africa, and forms the basis of a sound racial policy."[11]

This "debauching of religion to dulcify an abused people," Haselden affirms, is being continued yet today in more subtle ways with no scruples of conscience. This is best illustrated, he suggests, by the white man's use of the phrase "a good Negro." The connotation of the word "good" is completely different than it would be if it were prefixed before "white man." The Christian gentleman of the majority race has appropriated the positive adjectives for himself: "noble, manly, wise, strong, courageous." For the Negro he reserves the passive and negative virtues: patient, long-suffering, self-effacing, submissive, childlike. It becomes clear that in the definition of the white man "a good Negro" is an inoffensive Negro—one who is deferential in the presence of white people. "A bad Negro" would be one who is self-assured, bold, and ready to claim his rights as a citizen of a democracy.[12]

Far too long has the church been guilty of teaching a double standard of morality by reserving some of the Christian virtues exclusively for the dominant group and recommending others related to submission and meekness for the minority group. The church also, according to Haselden, has sinned by distorting the Christian ethic with an overemphasis on the other-worldly aspect of Christianity or by concentrating on the morality of the individual rather than being concerned with social problems. It may not be a coincidence, he hints, that "in America as in the Union of South Africa

[10] Haselden, *op. cit.,* p. 35.
[11] Cf. Moellering, *op. cit.,* p. 8.
[12] Haselden, *op. cit.,* pp. 41-46 .

the extremes of pietism and racial discrimination occupy the same territory." Religion and social problems are put in separate compartments and no relation between the two is admitted. Some "Bible belt" Christians may display genuine compassion and charity in their treatment of individual Negroes, but they are incapable of protesting against the existing social order which shields all sorts of inequities and abuses.[13]

Even worse is the way in which representatives of the Christian church have used biblical arguments to "prove" that Negroes are naturally inferior and predestined to be slaves or servants. As a result some whites have assumed that they have a Christian sanction for the contempt which they have for the personality of the Negro. Otherwise morally respectable people have judged their own "racial behavior, not as a fault, but rather as a faithful performance of the Christian ethic." People have developed, Haselden shows on the basis of questionnaires, "a deep-seated, mystical, religious abhorrence of social contact between Negroes and whites." The conviction has arisen that the association of the races on all levels of equality would somehow dishonor God and be morally objectionable. Sadly enough, a distorted concept of Christian morality has become a stumbling block to the acceptance of racial integration. So the church must be blamed for being a "teacher of immoral moralities."[14]

The Dutch Reformed church in South Africa has expended men and money in evangelizing the colored natives. Mission stations have been staffed with white *predikants,* and schools with good equipment and high standards have been built. "But it is always with the conviction," as Trevor Huddleston reported, "that somehow in the eternal purposes of Providence the white race is to *lead* the black: the black race is to depend upon . . . to *need* the white." According to the doctrine of total apartheid the day is anticipated when all earthly contact between black and white Christians will

[13] Cf. *ibid.,* pp. 47-50.
[14] Cf. *ibid.,* pp. 51-55.

become unnecessary. By its endorsement of the morality of segregation the church in South Africa has become "a tremendously strong predisposing factor" in upholding the cruelly restrictive racial policies of the government.[15]

Some American churches, sometimes unwillingly, have been giving the same moral sanction to the exploitation of minority groups. If they have not taught directly that Negroes should be content with their inferior status they have helped to preserve "separate, but *un*equal" facilities by supporting segregated schools, missions, or other institutions. Perhaps they have even deceived themselves into believing that they should be commended for their generous philanthropy.

In the spring of 1960, violence erupted in Capetown and Johannesburg. Mobs rioted, the despised passbook laws were flaunted, Negro leaders were imprisoned, and casualties were counted. With blind stubbornness and with disregard for the drive toward freedom which is sweeping over all Africa, the authorities appeared determined to pass even more stringent racial laws and seal their own eventual doom. The role of the Dutch Reformed church in these proceedings is a matter of record. Rather than assume the prophetic task and denounce oppression, the clergy have served as the morale boosters for the anti-Negro government policy, and scriptural "evidence" has been adduced to "prove" the inferiority of the natives and the moral rectitude of white domination. When Dr. Hendrik F. Verwoerd was elected Prime Minister in 1958, this champion of apartheid led the Afrikaner nationalists in singing an old Dutch hymn: "Let God's Blessings on Him Fall." According to his own statements Verwoerd fervently believes that God made the black to be in perpetuity a "hewer of wood and drawer of water" for the white man. He insists: "We are Christians and we attempt to do right." How could such a distorted view of Christian morality prevail without the endorsement of the church? Once

[15] Cf. Trevor Huddleston, *Naught for Your Comfort* (New York: Doubleday, 1956), pp. 66, 67.

again we are confronted with the sorry spectacle of the church bolstering the erring conscience of political leaders who are concealing their selfish aims under a Christian cloak.

Early in the fall of 1963 the editors of *Newsweek* welded the old art of journalism and the new science of public-opinion analysis to explore white reactions to the Negro revolt. They found a confusing ambivalence in the responses given. Unable to rid himself of his emotional bias against black skin, his profession of democratic ideals nevertheless compelled the white man to give verbal endorsement to equal rights for everyone. The white image of the Negro, "cruelly blurred by prejudice," was disclosed as an implausible and contradictory caricature, "half Stepin Fetchit—lazy, unwashed, shiftless, unambitious, slow-moving—and half Sportin' Life —cunning, lewd, flashy, strong, fearless, immoral, and vicious." For the most part, whites admitted that Negroes had been the victims of prejudice and they were prepared to make concessions, but they were still unwilling to be pushed too far and too fast.

Ready to agree that Negroes should be entitled to improved housing, they were opposed to any federal law that could enforce integrated housing. A substantial majority of whites were reconciled to the inevitability of desegregation in schools and public accommodations, but they did not want to accept them as personal friends or next-door neighbors.[16]

Spokesmen from the South still express resentment over "interference" from the federal government and the NAACP. Not infrequently, self-acclaimed "moderates" voice their judgment that Negroes are harming "their own cause" by pressing their demands too vehemently. Appeals are made for a more mild approach. Our social customs, it is urged, cannot be breached in a month, a year, or perhaps in a generation.

This "go slow" viewpoint has usually been reflected in the churches. Cautious Christians, traditionally skeptical of any movement that recommends aggressive action, have espoused "gradual-

[16] Cf. *Newsweek* (October 21, 1963), pp. 44-55.

ism"—pleading that we must deal gently with the "weak" (prejudiced?) brethren. As a matter of fact "gradualism" too often has been seized upon as a convenient excuse for stalling or doing nothing at all.

The issue which should be faced by Christians everywhere might be phrased in these terms: Which strategy for progress imposes the greatest hardship? Who makes the greater sacrifice, the white northerner who loses money in a real estate investment, or the Negro who continues to live in a congested neighborhood where his health is impaired and his children are denied equal educational opportunity? Which of us faces the harder task, the white southerner who would revamp his thinking and his social mores so drastically, or the millions of Negroes in Alabama or Mississippi who must endure restrictions and indignities for another generation or two? It is easy to preach patience and submission when you are a member of the privileged majority. Is it not time that we urge the white man to "take up his cross" and follow Christ instead of merely commending the plodding Negro who does not collapse under the burden imposed upon him? Why should the church move at a snail's pace because some of its members threaten to withdraw if Negroes are admitted? Is the purpose of the church to accumulate large numbers of "satisfied customers" who are effectively shielded from disturbances in society? Why should ministers evince so much concern for the beleaguered southern "gentlemen" who may lose some of their exclusive privileges, and so little genuine sympathy for the plight of the exploited and oppressed?

Meanwhile, leadership in the crusade to acquire full dignity and first class citizenship for minorities has already shifted to the Negro people. Young Negroes, especially intelligent students, are not "pulling punches" in making known their dissatisfaction with a policy of "gradualism" that would condemn their own generation and the next to inferiority and deprivation. Most disconcerting to the Ku Klux Klaners and the white "bullies" who would resort to strong-arm tactics is the unwillingness of the Negro community to be intimidated any longer. "We are not afraid" is the chant repeated by Negroes at their rallies or when they are facing imprisonment.

Negro churchmen have been in the vanguard of the struggle for human rights. Where have the white clergy been? At a safe distance in the North many noble resolutions have been passed by church conferences. A few courageous voices in the South have spoken at grave personal peril. But, for the most part, the churches continue to lag behind secular agencies on what is indubitably a moral issue of the utmost importance. The Koinonia colony at Americus, Georgia, seeking to emulate the early community of Christians at Jerusalem, has been persecuted and boycotted because of its interracial constituency. Christian churches in the area have surrendered to the bias and animus of their members and have declined to offer assistance in any way.

One of the results of the new developments in the South has been the insulation of the white community. By and large they are unaware of the real sentiments and aspirations of the Negro people. They have deluded themselves so long with wishful fantasies about how Negroes are contented with their inferior status that they refuse to face grim realities. One Lutheran minister in Montgomery gave heroic assistance to the bus boycott at the cost of having his home bombed three times and the lives of his wife and children endangered. But he was the rare exception. More typical was the white minister who appeared at the national institute of the Lutheran Human Relations Association of America to argue that Negroes in Alabama were perfectly satisfied with their lot, and there would have been no disturbance at all if it had not been for the presence of troublemakers from the outside.

The adverse effect of racial sins in American churches on our missionary enterprises abroad has been reported from many reliable sources. When the globe-trotting Billy Graham returned to this country from an evangelistic tour of Africa he emphasized that "Christianity's biggest stumbling block" in seeking to gain converts in "pagan" lands is the spreading awareness on the part of native leaders that many church groups in America are segregated: "They can't believe it. They can't take it. They're astounded to hear that Christian institutions bar a man on the basis of color. . . . If American churches are to render effective missionary help in Africa they are going to have to rethink their own segregation politics . . . 70% of the world is colored."[17]

Another way to gauge the performance of the Christian church in race relations is to check its rating in some of our contemporary fiction.

The tragic consequences of sustaining an extremely tight barrier between the races with legal penalties and religious scruples is illustrated by the fate of the leading characters in Alan Paton's novel, *Too Late the Phalarope.* When the lieutenant is frustrated by his wife's frigidity, overcome by his "mad sickness," and enters into an illicit relationship with a colored girl, he is not only guilty of adultery, but he is accused of violating the Immorality Act of the Union of South Africa. Marital infidelity among the Afrikaners would be pardonable, perhaps even winked at. But to have crossed the color line is the unforgiveable sin. The lieutenant is sentenced to prison. His career is ruined. His whole family is disgraced. His wife and children must move away. His youngest sister must break her engagement and go into seclusion. His married sisters try to forget their maiden names. His impeccable father crosses out the name of his own offspring from the family Bible, applies the words of an imprecatory psalm (109) to his reprobate son, and dies shortly afterwards from a stroke.[18] Everyone was "destroyed" because the church in South Africa had become a "teacher of immoral moralities."

In many American novels written by Negroes or about Negro-white relations the Christian church is depicted as "the purveyor of

[17] Moellering, *op. cit.*, p. 9.

[18] Alan Paton, *Too Late the Phalarope* (New York: Charles Scribner's Sons, 1953). See especially pp. 54, 55, 228, 239-72.

arrant sedatives" or as an irrelevant, if not ludicrous sideshow, to the big issues of life. In the autobiography of his childhood and youth Richard Wright tells how he was disturbed by the struggles of his people and the "meaningless suffering" which he saw on every hand. The religious practices of the Negroes seemed to be superstitions diverting their attention from the need for social justice. His grandmother with whom he lived was an ardent member of the Seventh-day Adventist church. He recalls:

> I was compelled to make a pretense of worshiping her God, which was her exaction for my keep. The elders of her church expounded a gospel clogged with images of vast lakes of eternal fire, of seas vanishing, of valleys of dry bones, of the sun burning to ashes, of the moon turning to blood, of stars falling to the earth, of a wooden staff being transformed into a serpent, of voices speaking out of clouds, of men walking upon water, of God riding whirlwinds, of water changing into wine, of the dead rising and living, of the blind seeing, of the lame walking; a salvation that teemed with fantastic beasts having multiple heads and horns and eyes and feet; sermons of statues possessing heads of gold, shoulders of silver, legs of brass, and feet of clay; a cosmic tale that began before time and ended with the clouds of the sky rolling away at the Second Coming of Christ; chronicles that concluded with the Armageddon; dramas thronged with all the billions of human beings who had ever lived or died as God judged the quick and the dead . . . .
>
> While listening to the vivid language of the sermons I was pulled toward emotional belief, but as soon as I went out of the church and saw the bright sunshine and felt the throbbing life of the people in the streets I knew that none of it was true and that nothing would happen.
>
> Once again I knew hunger, biting hunger, . . .[19]

As Negroes migrate North and become urbanized and surrounded by a materialistic culture, some of them tend to lose their religious moorings. As they become absorbed in raising their economic level, television, new automobiles, and the latest gadgets produced by

[19] Richard Wright, *Black Boy* (New York: Harper, 1937), p. 89.

technological America become objects of highest value. The church loses its role as a medium for sociability and entertainment. As Negroes become more sophisticated they may seek to emancipate themselves from the crude simplicities of the religion they knew in the South. In revolt against emotional excesses, and too enlightened to accept the extreme literalism of an illiterate clergy, they may be inclined to emulate the bad example of secular-minded white citizens and renounce all religious ties or become "nominal Christians," who have lost any genuine interest in the church. Few are likely to be openly hostile to Christianity. Some may resent its failure to practice the love which it professes. More are likely to become indifferent and simply regard the churches as irrelevant to their new interests. Their childhood memory of their parental church may be that of tediously prolonged worship or of compulsory Sunday school attendance.

In her searing story of how the black and white worlds collided in a New England town, Ann Petry describes a handsome, intelligent young Negro who was orphaned and raised by a respectable, churchgoing widow. When the boy Link is invited by the owner of the Last Chance tavern to come down to the dock on Sunday and learn how to swim,

> Link thanked him though he knew that it wasn't possible because he had to go to Sunday School, and to church, with Abbie because Abbie was superintendent of the Sunday School, and they had to set an example for the other colored people, so even if it rained or snowed, they went just the same.[20]

When Link was a grown man his erstwhile guardian Abbie remonstrated with him because he no longer went to church. Then he recalled:

> He'd gone plenty when he was a kid, enough to last him the rest of his life. He could remember how church ate the heart, the life out

[20] Ann Petry, *The Narrows* (New York: Signet Books, 1953), p. 128.

> of Sundays. He could see himself, washed and scrubbed and carrying a Bible, walking always within hand's reach of the white gloves Abbie wore. She carried a Bible too. They walked side by side, the straightbacked, smallboned woman and the reluctant boy, the carriers of Bibles. And down at the other end of Dumble Street, in the opposite direction, was the river. Every kid he knew was on the dock, near the dock, around the dock, drying off, sunning himself, diving in, swimming, loafing. And he, in Sunday School, and then in church, and the new minister's prayers were so long, so long, he closed his eyes and tried not to think, to go to sleep, and the voice went on and on, "Look down on us poor sinners, help us, Oh, Lord—"[21]

To break the monotony he would try to count the panes in the nearest stained-glass windows or the light bulbs in the chandeliers. One time he deliberately dropped his hymnal. Sometimes he would amuse himself by imagining that he was declaring war

> on Abbie, the minister, the old ladies dozing in the front pews, the old men who sat in the back pews leaning on their canes, the choir. He would shoot the soprano just at dawn, she had a quaver in her voice and buck teeth, and was always poking at him with her foot. Then he was God and all the angels, he was Gabriel blowing on a horn, blowing for the Judgment, and he was Ezekiel and he saw a wheel and a wheel and wheels, he was Moses leading his people to the Promised Land, booting his people to the Promised Land.[22]

In one of the flashbacks to his childhood Link remembered how the only colored Catholic in The Narrows had spoken her prayers in French when she was dying.

> For a long time afterwards, he had wondered how God, whom he has always assumed to be a Protestant and an American, had been able to understand her. . . .[23]

In Lillian Smith's *Strange Fruit* the setting is a Georgia town where a prolonged religious revival is in progress. The sins against

[21] *Ibid.*, p. 61. [22] *Ibid.*, p. 62. [23] *Ibid.*, p. 160.

which the preacher rants and raves are drunkenness, gambling, stealing, and other personal vices. There is no application whatsoever to the social ills that beset the community. By outward profession the townspeople are devout Christians. Only the newspaper editor does not conform with the behavior pattern expected from all respectable citizens of praying, hymn-singing, and church-going; and he is not ready to risk his business by speaking or writing anything contrary to "the southern way of life."

When a white man is murdered by the enraged brother of the colored concubine he has impregnated, this "Christian" community loses whatever sanity and sense of decency it once had. The double standard ethic of white Christians is displayed in its most gruesome aspect. The "code of the South" has been violated and someone must pay the penalty. The real Negro assailant has escaped to the North, but this does not prevent an infuriated mob from seizing an innocent suspect and burning him in a frenzy of public passions. The deepest pathos of the story is found in the connivance or approval of the very people who had just been "saved" or reconverted in the excitement of the revival. One may wonder if there is really very much difference between the emotional release that the crowd gained from listening to the hellfire preaching and from burning the "dirty Nigger."[24]

Then there are the more fastidious "Christians" who would not approve of lynching, but who are cowed into silence. One of the characters says: "Everybody's scared. . . . White man's blown himself up to such a size, now his own shadow scares him. Scared to do the decent thing for fear it will only do—harm."[25]

[24] Cf. Lillian Smith, *Strange Fruit* (New York: Reynal and Hitchcock, 1944), p. 357: " 'Thing that got me most,' Charley said slowly, 'was the hate on folks' faces. Even on the women's. . . . Some of those men were at that revival last night at the altar . . . praying to be saved. This afternoon they burned a man to ash.' " Used by permission of Harcourt, Brace and World.

[25] *Ibid.,* p. 356. Cf. p. 361 another character muses: "Well, he'd keep out of it himself, for a lynching wasn't to his liking. One of those things that seemed necessary now and then, but you let the other fellow do it. Like sticking a pig—much as you liked your cracklin' bread, you couldn't stand a hog-killing. Just hoped they got the right nigger. Maybe they did. Maybe they didn't."

As Tom Harris, who wants to befriend the Negro, sits at home lamenting the horrible episode, his son Charlie remarks:

> "Sometimes, Dad, when I think of the South all I can see is a white man kneeling on a nigger's stomach. Every time he raises his arms in prayer he presses a little deeper in the black man's belly. . . . Trouble is, you can't be a Christian in the South. You can't be one even if you want to, in the setup we've got down here! Everybody gouging his living out of somebody beneath him—singing hymns as he gouges."[26]

The picture which novelist Lillian Smith draws of Brother Dunwoodie is not complimentary to the Christian ministry. His chief regret about the lynching seems to be that it will cut down attendance at the revival meetings for a while. With a proper expression of righteous indignation he asserts privately to his fellow evangelist that he cannot condone what has happened. Brother Saunders agrees, but adds the consoling thought:

> "But it doesn't do any good to criticize people—not at a time like this. Only stirs up more bad feeling between the races. It don't do to *talk* about these things. Makes them worse! Now it's always been my policy to keep out of controversies and politics. A servant of God has no business mixing in such matters. Our job is the winning of souls to Christ."[27]

Earlier in the narrative preacher Dunwoodie is called upon to counsel the wayward Tracy whose parents suspect that he has been visiting colored town for nocturnal rendezvous with Nonnie Anderson, an attractive, college-educated Negro woman. His family and the minister are willing to settle for a feigned conversion to the Christian faith and an outward show of respectability. The crucial thing is that he give up the colored girl, even though she is going to bear his child. Brother Dunwoodie has a different moral code for this embarrassing situation than the moral code he preaches for

[26] *Ibid.*, pp. 354, 355. [27] *Ibid.*, p. 358.

white people. He is aware that illicit sexual relations across the color line, initiated by white men, are quite common. But he expects that the merciful Lord will be quite lenient when judging these more trivial lapses of youth. His advice to the worried Tracy is:

> "Fix things! Find some good nigger you can count on to marry her. Give her some money. . . . There's a lot of important folks on your side . . . and God's among them. Don't forget that."[28]

In his travel memoirs, the Reverend Clemonce Sabourin tells of the inconveniences and indignities which he met on a trip through the South with his wife and young boy. All along the route from New York to Florida, and beyond toward New Orleans, he observed a most feverish religious activity. The farther South he went the more signs he saw advertising the churches: "Jesus Saves," "Christ is the Answer," "Go to Church." He could not help but be struck by the contradiction between this widely professed allegiance to Christianity and the treatment accorded the Negro population.[29]

In New Orleans Pastor Sabourin had a conversation with a Negro insurance agent in which the man said that the white people looked upon Negroes as dogs and the new school buildings being constructed for the colored were the crumbs falling from the master's table. Then when Sabourin inquired if the man was a Christian he received this reply:

> "Well . . . yes," he said . . . "at least, I was. . . . I became a Catholic. But it didn't do any good. It didn't bring me any closer to Catholics—not white ones, anyway. I know the teachings of the Church. I know the fine statements made by high Catholic officials; Protestants, too. But the man in the pulpit isn't opening his mouth. Catholics and Protestants alike go right on discriminating, go right on sweating

[28] *Ibid.*, p. 100.

[29] Cf. Clemonce Sabourin, *Let the Righteous Speak* (New York: Pageant 1957), pp. 12, 25 ff.

your blood out, go right on letting any white man, even if he is as sinful as Satan, spit on any colored man, even if he is as holy as Mary. When I became a Catholic I thought I would find peace. But if there is any peace of God that passes all understanding, I didn't find it. The little peace I found was kicked right out of me by my fellow Christians. I had become a Catholic, but I hadn't become a human being. I had become a Catholic, but I was only a black Catholic, just as you are a black Lutheran . . . and neither of us will ever be accepted as anything more. . . ."[30]

While Pastor Sabourin was staying overnight in a Negro motel in Birmingham, Alabama, he entered into a prolonged discussion with a native who freely expressed his views on school integration. He explained that Negro children might not always be able to compete with their white schoolmates because of poor home environment, and pointed out that the whole system of segregation is blameworthy. Sabourin interrupted to remark that if a change is to be made it must begin with a transformation of the heart, and at this point, he suggested, the clergy should be expected to perform their duty. He remembered that he had seen hundreds of churches in the South. With all of these Catholic priests and Protestant ministers preaching Christian truth and love, it would seem that their white listeners could not fail to develop a more sympathetic understanding of the Negro's plight. To this end the little man responded:

"Look, friend, don't put your faith in clergymen. If they really wanted to do something, they could. But how many of them want to? Why, I once saw a preacher throw a rock at a Negro boy. With my own ears I heard him call that Negro boy a little black bastard. . . . Even the best of them meet in conferences and pass innocuous resolutions; but when they stand in their own pulpits on Sunday morning, they're dumb. They preach sermons about the forgiveness of sins, but they never say that treating Negroes like you would not want to be treated is a sin."[31]

[30] *Ibid.*, p. 48.
[31] *Ibid.*, p. 65.

The little man went on to say that no one respected the clergy as spiritual leaders. They were only regarded as the presidents of social organizations. When Mr. Sabourin protested that at least "the man in the pulpit has the ear of his people . . ." his new acquaintance bristled to retort:

> "I know! . . . What good does it do? He says what the people want to hear. And even if he did preach against the evils of segregation, do you think it would do any good? I tell you, nobody respects the Church, not even the devout members who attend. Look! Suppose a preacher began hammering away at the evils of segregation. First thing, his members would tell him to preach the Gospel and let the race problem alone. If he didn't stop, they might ride his tail out of town. Does that sound like respect? If he kept it up and stuck to his pulpit, they still wouldn't pay any attention to him. Why? It's because the Church never has been bound by segregation laws. If the Church wanted to, the Church could have integrated its congregations, its schools, its Sunday schools, all the way down the line. That could have been done fifty years ago, a hundred years ago. But the clergy didn't tell the people to do it. Now, when they talk about it, the people say if segregation is an evil today, it was an evil fifty years ago. Why didn't you tells us then? It it wasn't evil then, why do you talk about it now? . . . And what can the preachers answer? . . . You can't respect that kind of clergy."[32]

In a book called *Dark Symphony,* Elizabeth Laura Adams tells about her spiritual odyssey that eventually led her to the bosom of Rome. Midway in the story, when she and her mother had moved to a place where they could not affiliate with a Negro church, she began to attend one with a solemn liturgical service which appealed to her. In response to the cordial invitation of the minister she and her mother became regular members. Soon afterward they moved to another town, found a church of the same denomination, and presented their letter of recommendation for membership. Miss Adams recalls that she worshiped faithfully and listened attentively to the zealous preaching of the clergyman in which he often re-

[32] *Ibid.*, p. 66.

peated that "Jesus died to save all mankind!" One Sunday morning as she and her mother knelt at the communion rail she was startled to notice that the minister was briskly wiping the chalice after their lips had touched it before he served the next white communicant. He appeared to make the cleansing operation as obvious as possible to the congregation, and Miss Adams was terrified with the thought which she says flashed through her mind like a newspaper headline: RACE PREJUDICE AT THE ALTAR. Then she regretted having such a sinful thought in such a holy place, and she begged God for forgiveness. But during the next week the white minister came to see them:

> He stated his mission, tears filling his eyes and streaming down his cheeks. He informed us that White communicants did not wish to kneel at the altar with Negroes . . . he regretted having to tell us . . . he hoped that we would not hate him . . . but he had to make a living . . . White people contributed so much to the church . . . he had more White parishioners than Colored.[33]

Negro author, James Baldwin, has written about his "spiritual seduction" and involvement "in the church racket." His vision of God, he confesses, has always been "white." To many Christians, he realizes, he is "a descendant of Ham" who has been cursed and predestined to slavery. In his younger days when he faced a congregation, he recalls:

> It began to take all the strength I had not to stammer, not to curse, not to tell them to throw away their Bibles and get off their knees and go home and organize . . . a rent strike. . . . I felt that I was committing a crime in talking about the gentle Jesus, in telling them to reconcile themselves to their misery on earth in order to gain the crown of eternal life. . . . There was no love in the church. It was a mask for hatred and self-hatred and despair.[34]

[33] Elizabeth Laura Adams, *Dark Symphony* (New York: Sheed and Ward, 1942), pp. 125, 126.

[34] James Baldwin, *The Fire Next Time* (New York: Dial Press, 1963), pp. 43-45, 50, 53. Copyright © 1963, 1962 by James Baldwin.

Christianity, Baldwin asserts, has become identified with the virtue and power of the white man. Dr. Verwoerd of South Africa is convinced that God is on the side of the Afrikaners. But the Black Muslims sing to calypso music: "The white man's heaven is the black man's hell." When the imperialists came to Africa, these Negro supremacists say "the white man had the Bible and the African had the land. But now it is the white man who is being reluctantly and bloodily separated from the land, and the African who is still attempting to digest or to vomit up the Bible." "The Christian church," Baldwin agrees, "sanctified and rejoiced in the conquests of the flag" and encouraged the rationalization that the material gains of the West were proof of God's benediction. "Whoever wishes to become a truly moral human being," says this acid-tongued critic representative of the new Negro belligerency, "must first divorce himself from all the prohibitions, crimes, and hypocrisies of the Christian Church."[35]

Harriet Harmon Dexter once complained that we had been hearing too much bad news about racial tensions, so, in 1958, she wrote a book to tell us *What's Right with Race Relations.* On many fronts she was able to report encouraging progress, but there is little in her chapter on the "Churches Accept Responsibility" to evoke jubilation. Despite her strained effort to accentuate the positive and gloss over the miserable failure of the churches with a description of extenuating circumstances, one can read between the lines and imagine that he sees written "too little too late." One is forced to conclude that to illustrate her theme it might have been best if she had omitted all reference to the American churches.[36]

To give a full picture of a generally regrettable situation, however, it should be admitted that there have been some signs that the churches have not entirely abandoned their redemptive task. Ne-

[35] *Ibid.*, pp. 59-61.

[36] Harriet Harmon Dexter, *What's Right with Race Relations* (New York: Harper, 1958). A condensed version appeared in *Pulpit Digest* (January, 1959), pp. 41-43.

groes were included in the humanitarian outreach of the churches. After making full allowance for the dubious motivation involved in some of the charities for Negroes (a substitute for social justice used to appease the conscience?), the undeniable fact remains that Protestant churches did considerable work in improving the educational and health standards of their underprivileged neighbors of another color. The record of the Federal Council of Churches was consistently honorable. In the tension-filled year of 1919 the Administrative Committee issued a special eight-point appeal calling for protection from mob violence; equal job opportunity; maintenance of the sanctity of the Negro home; access to equal traveling, educational, and recreational facilities; the implementation of voting rights; and closer cooperation between the races. Repeatedly in the 1930's the Council made itself heard on the Negro question, especially in regard to the practice of segregation at church conferences. In 1921 a Commission on the Church and Race Relations was organized which proposed the observance of a Race Relations Sunday and a Brotherhood Month. Northern Methodism also assumed a rather progressive position on the Negro issue. In 1924 its General Conference adopted a resolution introduced by E. Stanley Jones rejecting as "unchristian and untrue the idea that certain races are born to inherent and fixed superiority and rulership, while others are born to inherent and fixed inferiority and subordination." The opening year of the "depression decade" found the Northern Baptist Convention condemning race prejudice as the greatest obstacle to the establishment of the kingdom of God on earth. By 1939 even the Southern Baptist Convention adopted a vigorous resolution calling for the termination of racial inequality. Particularly influential in arousing the conscience of American Christendom were the courageous and candid editorials which have appeared in the pages of the *Christian Century*.[37]

In 1936 the Georgia-Alabama Synod of the United Lutheran

[37] Cf. Robert Moats Miller, *Protestantism and Social Issues, 1919-1939* (Chapel Hill: University of North Carolina Press, 1958), pp. 302-12.

Church in America petitioned the national convention for an expansion of mission outreach among southern Negroes. What was envisioned was the creation of a separate Negro Synod in the South. The request was declined by the assembled body due to a lack of Negro clergy.

The incident was recalled by Malcolm Aage Jackson in an article written in 1940 on "The Negro and the U.L.C." with the plea:

> It is high time that the U.L.C. address itself to a program of putting an end to conditions and attitudes toward Negroes that are incompatible with Christian teachings, so that an infiltration of new blood into this denomination will show its universality and prove its finer sentiments.[38]

Mr. Jackson felt that "the rank and file of Americans" are "condescending and misinformed on the subject of the Negro." He deplored the fact that leaders of denominations have often condoned the practice of segregation which predominates in most of the country:

> They have advocated and perpetuated separate synods, because they were too narrow and provincial to worship at the fountain of universal brotherhood. And so eight million Negroes are left unchurched and uncared for because traditions and selfish thoughts are more strongly respected than Christ's teachings.[39]

The Negro, Jackson intimates, cannot help but reflect on the anomaly that Protestant churches are disturbed by the imprisonment of Niemoeller and religious persecution in Russia, but are completely unperturbed by the plight of Negroes in America. It does not make much sense to pretend that we are eager to save "the heathen in darkest Africa," when in our own country we are denying basic rights and economic well being to a whole race of people.

[38] *Lutheran Church Quarterly,* XIII (October, 1940), 416. [39] *Ibid.*

Segregation in the church is unthinkable. Christ did not preach "to white men in one place and black men in the other." Lutheranism, if it is to perform its duty, must not procrastinate in actively soliciting Negro members. Of course, the Lutheran church cannot expect to gain many Negro followers until it has demonstrated a sincere interest in helping the Negro acquire his social and political rights. "The U.L.C.A. cannot hide behind the principle that the time is not ripe for the Negro's absorption; nor can it wait patiently for him to come running to its bosom."[40]

If one is searching for a really bright spot in the history of American Christianity, none more brilliant can be found than the heroic role played by Negro clergy and Negro churches in the Montgomery bus boycott. Unfortunately it must be added that, aside from a few outstanding exceptions, the Caucasian ministers of that city were unwilling to risk their personal safety by supporting this bid for freedom. Some even held membership in the White Citizens Councils that tried to keep the Negroes in subjection. Yet the fact remains that, for once, outstanding Christian leadership was boldly exerted; the ethics of Jesus were taken seriously, applied consistently, and proved effective. Christian "idealism" became demonstrably practical. The virtues of humility, non-resistance to evil, and love for one's enemies were used not to promote a passive compliance with abusive restrictions that trampled on human dignity. They were converted into potent "weapons" for achieving a resounding victory over racial discrimination in the public transportation system of a city in the Deep South.[41]

While due credit for this achievement must be given to Dr. Martin Luther King for his dynamic leadership, one must also admire the courage and persistence of all the participants. Any misstep could have led to bloodshed and violence. The Negro clergy and churches used prayer and all the spiritual resources at their

[40] *Ibid.*, p. 417.

[41] Cf. Martin Luther King, *Stride Toward Freedom* (New York: Harper, 1958).

disposal to prevent outbursts of hatred or ill-advised actions that might have discredited the movement. At the same time, underlying the whole movement, there was an unyielding conviction among the Negro people that as Christians and creatures of God they deserved to be treated like decent human beings and not like inferiors or the scum of the earth. This crusade for social justice was undertaken in the name of Christ and is an unmistakable illustration of what Kyle Haselden means when he writes:

> One and the same Gospel will not forever comfort one people in their claim to superiority and content another people in their status of oppression and servitude.[42]

While white Christians, by using their religion to tame the protesting Negro, have given credence to the Communist assault on the church,

> Negro Christians who will not be deceived, who insist upon their full humanity, whose religion itself requires that they respect themselves as a part of sacred life and that they be complete rather than partial persons, have the honor of denying the Marxist denunciation of all religion.[43]

An honest and comprehensive appraisal of the performance of American Protestantism can only yield a negative and reprimanding judgment. By default American Christianity has failed to perform its prophetic mission and counteract the forces of oppression.

"Truly I perceive that God shows no partiality, but in every nation any one who fears him and does what is right is acceptable to him" (Acts 10:35). "But if you show partiality you commit sin, and are convicted by the law as transgressors" (Jas. 2:9). "If we say we have no sin, we deceive ourselves, and the truth is not in us. If we confess our sins, he is faithful and just, and will

[42] Haselden, *op. cit.,* p. 39.
[43] *Ibid.,* p. 45.

forgive our sins and cleanse us from all unrighteousness" (I John 1:8, 9).

The application of these verses to the church's record in race relations should be self-evident. As long as complacency and self-satisfaction are the predominant mood among clergy and laity there can be little hope that our performance in the next fifty years will be any more praiseworthy. The first step toward improvement must be self-examination and repentance. After we have admitted our sins of commission and omission we can proceed to remedy the situation with more sincerity and enthusiasm.

8 The Guilty Conscience and the Dread of Racial Intermarriage

The issue which invariably is raised by Caucasians in any discussion about multiplying interracial contacts is the question of "mixed" marriages. The most dreaded consequence of preaching racial equality or of proceeding with integration in the church is the presumption that it will lead to sexual intercourse or marriage between whites and blacks. Abraham Lincoln agreed with his debate opponent, Stephen A. Douglas, that "the mixing of blood by the white and black races" was a repulsive thought.[1] The original leader of the White Citizens Councils in Mississippi said: "I, for one, would gladly lay down my life to prevent mongrelization. There is no greater cause."[2]

The extensive *Newsweek* poll conducted in 1963 on "What the White Man Thinks of the Negro Revolt" indicated that whites were almost unanimous in their disapproval of interracial dating. Ninety percent of the people interviewed said they would be disturbed if their teen-ager kept close company with a Negro of the

[1] See Milton Mayer, "The Issue is Miscegenation," *The Progressive* (September, 1959), p. 156.

[2] John Bartlow Martin, *The Deep South Says Never* (New York: Ballantine, 1957), p. 2. Cf. Ralph L. Moellering, "What about Racial Intermarriage?" *American Lutheran,* XLIII (September, 1960), p. 14. Some of the material found in this chapter originally appeared in this article.

opposite sex. Even whites who are prepared to welcome Negroes to their offices, and are not averse to having them living next door, shrink away from the thought of the marriage altar. "Shaking hands is OK," remarked a man in San Diego, "but kissing—no thanks." An artist in Virginia City, Nevada, repeated the stereotype: "Negroes are oversexed. They're wild."[3]

Negroes in the South know that it is dangerous even to display any curiosity about the feminine features of an attractive white woman. Many of the lynchings, including one in Mississippi as recently as 1959, were provoked by instances in which Negro men were reported to have had illicit relations with white women. Because he allegedly whistled at a white woman, Emmett Till's body was brutally mangled and tortured. Although "rape" is not an uncommon crime, and it is not always clear whether the "victim" is entirely innocent, yet it becomes a monstrous offense if committed by a Negro against a white person. It is publicized as sensationally shocking news, and even capital punishment would not be sufficient to appease those who seek vengeance.

Clemonce Sabourin confesses in his book *Let the Righteous Speak:*

> As far as white women were concerned, I had trained myself to think blank. This was safe . . . this was my [place]. The white men could stare and comment and undress her with their eyes but in their presence, a black man had to see and yet not see, judge and yet have no opinion.[4]

Some of the most malicious literature imaginable has been peddled by hate mongers who appeal to inbred and irrational fears. A torrent of abusive epithets are hurled at the advocates of full racial freedom. The States Rights League of Tulsa, Oklahoma, intimates that the white race may disappear if segregation is not up-

[3] *Newsweek* (October 21, 1963), pp. 44-55.

[4] Clemonce Sabourin, *Let the Righteous Speak* (New York: Pageant, 1957), p. 49.

held, and advertises "a map of the Black Republic proposed by the mongrelizers and Communists to take up 12,000 square miles out of the heart of the Deep South."

An article featured in *The Cross and the Flag* under the name of Oscar Grow pleads for "racial fidelity" as the only guarantor for the preservation of the "Aryan" peoples. The one unmistakable lesson of history, he affirms, is that those nations which have transgressed against their racial purity have paid the price of inevitable decline and collapse. Swarming hordes of aliens, he argues, descended upon the great ancient civilizations of Egypt, Persia, Greece, and Rome; and, in each instance, racial tolerance "ended in amalgamation of all those diverse human elements into a motley conglomeration of human derelicts." The laws of nature cannot be broken with impunity. Sometimes, Mr. Grow declares, "the mongrel offspring is sterile and cannot perpetuate itself." Innate racial aversions and repulsive bodily odors are the Creator's way of compelling the races to live in seclusion from one another. According to this mode of thought racial prejudice is a virtue because it prevents us from sinning by crossing the racial barrier. Mr. Grow's arguments are typical of those used in pamphlets widely distributed throughout the South. Christian morality and contempt for other races is not irreconcilable because crossing the color line is always described as a symptom of moral degradation. Only a "morbid apostasy" can induce white people to seek the association of Negroes. Inferior races should not be "subsidized" by superior ones, but permitted to become extinct in the struggle for existence. "The most despicable traitor in the world is the racial traitor." "Miscegenation," the author concludes, "is genocide."

A kind of anti-Semitism which implicates the Zionist movement with the Communist conspiracy often indulges in tirades against the integrationists. A publication emanating from Parkesburg, Pennsylvania, uses a visual "scare" technique in depicting the evils of "hydra hybridiensis." The misshapen head of a repulsive-looking monster prefaces an article describing how the "One Worlders" are serving as the tools of the Kremlin and international Jewry in seeking to fuse the "colored element" with what is left of "our white pioneer stock." Unless this dismal trend which permits alien barbarians to pollute the purity of the race is reversed, the writer insists, western civilization is doomed.[5]

To fanatics, segregation has even become the primary manifestation of the divine will and an immutable law is designed to govern all of creation. A correspondent from Georgia remonstrates with the editors of the *Christian Century* for failing to recognize that racial intermarriage has always provoked the punitive justice of the Almighty God. "... the main cause of His sending the judgment of the flood was the sons of God (the righteous line of Seth) intermarrying with the unrighteous line of Cain." The Israelites were forbidden to intermarry with the Canaanites who were a mongrel race, but were commanded through Moses to exterminate them. The Supreme Court decision on school desegregation, the writer continues, was dictated by Satan, and everyone who favors it should be "cursed" with "the blackest Negro man this side of Africa for a son-in-law." This self-appointed "prophet" concludes by predicting that all integrationists who do not repent will be sentenced to eternal hellfire by "the Author of segregation."

The North is not free from this same kind of venom. The *Women's Voice,* published in Chicago by a woman with a Dutch name, and which blames the Jews for all the ills of mankind, joins the chorus denouncing integration. In one issue, J. B. Stone, who claims to represent "The Christian Party," argues against "the cult of equality" by trying to prove that there is a sharp line of demarcation indicated by the differences in physical features between Negroes and whites. From the description given, which includes comparisons with the ape and the gorilla, one gains the impression that the Negro is only half human; some of his bestial traits are still in evidence. Ignoring the fact that more than a hundred years have

[5] The original articles are in the files of the author. Cf. Moellering, *op. cit.,* p. 14.

elapsed since emancipation, proponents of Negro resettlement, like Mr. Stone, quote Abraham Lincoln's endorsement of some of the colonization schemes brought forward in his day. Christians, therefore, must defeat the Jew-Communist plot to rule a mongrel America by supporting the Langer Bill which would establish a homeland for American Negroes in Africa.

No doubt the time is long overdue for the Christian church to face forthrightly the repercussions and complications to be anticipated from increasing interracial romances and marriages, offer counsel and guidance to its members, and allow the biblical and historical testimony regarding the sanctity of sex and marriage to pervade society as a whole. It is futile and dangerous to be so squeamish that we regard the topic as too delicate for commentary. Neither in the church nor in the secular world is integration leading to a rapid increase in the number of interracial courtships and marriages. But if marriage between the races continues to be forbidden by law in some states, or frowned upon by "respectable people," we can expect more needless heartache, more illegitimate children, and more adultery.

Already our past sins of oppression are catching up with us. Someone has said that the white man's consternation over the prospect of freedom for sex relations between the races is caused by his guilty conscience. During the days of slavery and up to the present time he has been using his dominant position to take unfair advantage of Negro women. For white people, sexual exploitation of Negroes has been condoned and at times even encouraged, while a completely different moral code has been enforcd by law and custom when it comes to Negro offenses of the same kind.

During the American occupation of Germany, GI's took advantage of their release from taboos enforced in the States to "fraternize" with German girls. In October, 1946, *Ebony* devoted six pages to photographs showing *der Schwarz Amerikaner* and pretty German fräuleins in intimate associations at dances, in enlisted men's clubs, and on swimming parties. In December, 1947, *News-*

week reported on the pitiful plight of the "brown Tiny Tims" who were among the five thousand mulatto babies resulting from sex relations between Negro soldiers and English girls. No British adoption societies would accept the babies. American authorities would grant a visa to a child only if a GI admitted paternity, which he rarely did. Marriages were prohibited by War Department orders.

Britain, which outlawed slavery throughout the empire in 1833 and has long expressed pride over its record in race relations, was disturbed again by a wave of post-war colored immigration. By 1954 the Jamaican influx had reached flood proportions and the racial problem became acute. Although the chief cause of alarm was competition for jobs and housing, accusations involving prostitution and sexual offenses were made. Tabloids and magazines played up the sensational angles under such headlines as "Would You Let Your Daughter Marry a Negro?" When this writer led an interracial goodwill tour across eleven European countries in the summer of 1963, only in London did he find any expression of hostility toward non-whites. One of our taxicab drivers volunteered a tirade against people from the West Indies for lowering property values and indulging in prostitution.

More recently, white settlers across Africa from Cape Town to Nairobi have been chilled by fears of riot and rapine. In 1960 white women in the Belgian Congo received threatening phone calls intimating that when independence was achieved, they would be "adopted" for concubinage by the natives. Later in May of the same year the African newspaper *Notre Kongo* editorialized: "Until now it was African mothers who had to look after their mulatto offspring. . . . Now, the white woman will have to take care of mulattoes born from African men. . . . It is only just that things should change that way."

Another way to measure the dimensions of this problem is to see how it is reflected in the literature of our day. Current fiction is preoccupied with sex. Novels centering around the racial issue have often spun the intricacies of their plot around the tragic consequences of an interracial liaison. Graham Greene's *The Quiet American* has as a leading character the attractive Vietnamese girl, Phuon, who is the mistress of the English reporter, Thomas Fowler, and is wooed by the American intruder with honorable intentions, Aldyn Pyle. *Too Late the Phalarope* by Alan Paton is the episode of the young white police lieutenant who violates the inviolable code of his country when he meets a Negro girl by night. *The Lying Days* by Nadine Gordimer tells "about a young girl's awakening to womanhood and her flight from the conventional life in a small South Africa town." *A Grove of Fever Trees* by Daphne Rooke is a novel about "a strange English settlement on the African Thornveld, where a handsome, half-mad giant is stirred to savage violence by his love for a childhood sweetheart." *Look Not Upon Me* by Denys Jones is described as "a suspenseful story of forbidden love in the bloody Mau-Mau country." In Lillian Smith's *Strange Fruit,* Tracy, the white boy, is genuinely in love with the colored girl, Nonnie Anderson. But due to the rigid code of the Georgia town in which they live, they must meet furtively and make sin out of what, under favorable circumstances, could have been an honorable and happy marriage. In *The Narrows* by Ann Petry we are again presented with a situation in which black and white are irresistibly drawn together in a love affair. This time it is a wealthy, white heiress who finds relief from her loneliness in the arms of a Dartmouth-educated Negro.

In one of his short plays called *The Respectful Prostitute,* the French existentialist Jean-Paul Sartre unleashes a devastating attack on the hypocrisy of southern gentlemen. In the story two young men from prominent white families are drunk after celebrating a football victory. They board a train and make passes at Lizzie who is on her way from the North to a southern town to practice her art which is that of a prostitute. Under the influence of alcohol, and in their hilarious mood, the white men try to throw two Negroes out of the window. One fights back in self defense and punches one of the white men in the nose. Infuriated at the thought that a Negro dared to strike him physically, the white man draws a gun and kills him. The other Negro jumps off the train as it is coming into the station and escapes.

According to "good" southern tradition justice cannot be meted out to the guilty culprit whose father is a powerful figure in the Senate. The brother of the murderer pays a nocturnal visit to "the respectful prostitute," and then tries to seal her lips with alternate threats and promises. To testify "against a white man in behalf of a nigger" would be unthinkable. It must be remembered, as the senator points out, that there are degrees of truth. One level of truth might indicate that a white man was guilty of immorality and manslaughter. But there is another "truth" to be weighed in the balances. What about the relative worth of the two men? Negro life is cheap. One more or less will make little difference. For the sake of preserving the life of a "blue blooded" southerner the Negro is expendable. Sure, Fred tells Lizzie, "he put his hand under your skirt, he shot down a dirty nigger; so what? You do things like that without thinking; they don't count. Thomas is a leading citizen, that's what counts."[6]

When "the respectful prostitute" professes to be unable to follow this line of reasoning, the senator who must save the honor of his family name at all costs, intercedes and tries a new approach to put across this interpretation of morality. It is, he says, as though Uncle Sam were pleading with the prostitute to be sensible:

> "Lizzie, this Negro whom you are protecting, what good is he? Somehow or other he was born, God knows where. I nourished and raised him, and how does he pay me back? What does he do for me? nothing at all; he dawdles, he chisels, he sings, he buys pink and green suits. He is my son, and I love him as much as I do my other boys. But I ask you: does he live like a man? I would not even notice

[6] Jean-Paul Sartre, *No Exit and Three Other Plays* (New York: Vintage Books, 1958), p. 263.

> if he died. . . . The other one, this Thomas, has killed a Negro, and that's very bad. But I need him. He is a hundred-per-cent American, comes from one of our oldest families, has studied at Harvard, is an officer—I need officers—he employs two thousand workers in his factory—two thousand unemployed if he happened to die. He's a leader, a firm bulwark against the Communists, labor unions, and the Jews. His duty is to live, and yours is to preserve his life."[7]

Meanwhile, the panicky Negro who has been fleeing his white pursuers has found a temporary refuge in Lizzie's apartment. She hands him a revolver and suggests that, if they are cornered, he use it to plug the senator's son who got them into this mess. She realizes that if they so much as suspected that she had included a Negro among her "customers" his life would be forfeited too. But the Negro has been so conditioned by his whole association with the white man that he sees himself through the eyes of the white man and derogates his own humanity. Lizzie asks: "[Do they have] a right to bleed you like a pig just because they're white?" But the hapless Negro is paralyzed with fear at the mere suggestion that he might shoot "white folks," even to protect his own life. Even though he is completely innocent of any wrongdoing he admits to Lizzie that he feels guilty.[8]

In the end a Negro who had no connection with the incident at all is seized by a mob and lynched, the fleeing Negro is shot by Fred, and the senator's son (Fred) who is invulnerable because his ancestors "made this country" persuades Lizzie to becomes his mistress.

One of the most humiliating ways in which whites have treated Negroes is to emasculate them by making it a capital crime to exhibit any normal sexual response to the presence of white women, even if their actions are sexually provocative. This is part of the theme in Ralph Ellison's National Book Award winning novel, *The Invisible Man.* Often the white man is not even conscious of the

[7] *Ibid.*, p. 270.
[8] Cf. *ibid.*, pp. 274-78.

Negro as a fellow human being. In Lillian Smith's *Strange Fruit,* Ed Anderson looked toward the white drug store:

> White girls in cars blew horns, ordered cokes, laughed, crossed their legs, uncrossed them, stared through him as their line of vision passed his body. He was a black digit marked out by white chalk. He wasn't there on the sidewalk.[9]

In his boyhood days Ralph Ellison was invited to deliver an oration before a banquet attended by the leading white citizens of his community. First, he discovered he would have to join in a "battle royal" (boxing blindfolded) with other Negro boys. "The little shines" were rushed up front in the ballroom while the striptease act was still in progress. Surrounded by a sea of white faces they saw directly in front of them "a magnificent blonde—stark naked." Ellison writes:

> I felt a wave of irrational guilt and fear. My teeth chattered, my skin turned to goose flesh, my knees knocked. Yet I was strongly attracted and looked in spite of myself. . . . I wanted at one and the same time to run from the room, to sink through the floor, or go to her and cover her from my eyes and the eyes of the others with my body. . . .[10]

A novel by Roy Flannagan, appearing in 1932 under the title *Amber Satyr,* was reissued as a paperback in 1952 under the disconcerting title of *Luther.* The name refers to a bronze giant, a swamp Negro, proud of his Indian blood, who must resist the temptation of yielding to the allurements of a frustrated white wife of a neighboring farmer. The shocking injustice of the prevailing mores is underscored by Luther's helplessness in averting the impregnation of his own daughter by a despicable white scoundrel, while he does not dare to accede to the blandishments of a white woman

[9] Lillian Smith, *Strange Fruit* (New York: Reynal and Hitchcock, 1944) p. 8. Used by permission of Harcourt, Brace and World.

[10] Ralph Ellison, *The Invisible Man* (New York: Signet Books, 1953), p. 22.

who secretly writes "love letters" to him, inflames his passions with liquor, and torments him with her efforts to seduce him. Consider this passage:

> Luther knew that Benjo Sprouse had gotten Sis in trouble, but there was nothing to do about it. If he made trouble with the white man, it would not help Sis. If he caught Benjo Sprouse on the road some day and broke him in two it would not help Sis. It would hurt her, because the white men would hang him for it and there would be nobody to take care of Sis.[11]

In the explosive ending, the outraged husband discovers the "love letters" and joins his blameworthy brother Benjo in capturing the mulatto and unmercifully emptying a revolver into his stomach.[12]

One of Richard Wright's later novels, *The Long Dream,* is a highly literate outburst of anger with the same complaint—Negroes are the victims of the guilty conscience of the white man. Sexual exploitation is blended with political corruption in some revolting episodes and a blistering account of "man's inhumanity to man." Already, as a young boy, Fishbelly, the central figure, has the warning drummed into his consciousness: "Never look at a white woman!" Part of his indoctrination in preparation for manhood comes when his father exclaims:

> "When you in the presence of a white woman [sic] remember she means *death*! The white folks hate us, fight us, kill us, make laws against us; but they use this damned business about white women to make what they do sound right."[13]

Soon afterwards, a Negro hotel employee is caught in the room of a white woman who solicited his attentions. Under the pretense that he resisted arrest, he is not only murdered by white vengeance, but his body is lacerated and mutilated beyond all semblance of

[11] Roy Flannagan, *Luther* (New York: Lion, 1952), p. 43.

[12] Cf. Moellering, *op. cit.,* p. 19.

[13] Richard Wright, *The Long Dream* (New York: Ace, 1958), p. 60.

anything human. As the grieving mother bends over the mortal remains of her son she sobs hysterically:

> "Gawd, You didn't do this! You couldn't. And You got to do something to stop this from happening to black women's children! If I had to do it over again, I wouldn't have no child! I'd tear it out of my womb!"[14]

Richard Wright was, as his readers know, a cynical and bitter agnostic. (Cf. his book of essays entitled, *White Man, Listen!*) One underlying theme in *The Long Dream,* which is saturated with sex and violence, seems to be that the hypocrisy of the white man, and his insistence on shielding the white woman and placing her on a pedestal, only adds fuel to the fires of resentment, aggravates the breach between the races, and increases the curiosity of the Negro male. What is intimated is that if these artificial barriers were non-existent, the temptation to commit rape or sexual offenses would be diminished. While Fishbelly stands in the awe of the power wielded by the white man he cannot suppress the urge to contemplate what is forbidden:

> He was seeing that white waitress at the roadside soft-drink bazaar, seeing her red lips, the shimmying motion of her hips as she walked. . . . He knew deep in his heart that there would be no peace in his blood until he had defiantly violated the line that the white world had dared him to cross under the threat of death. . . . The threats designed to create fear in him had fostered a secret urging of hot desire.[15]

In a savage and nauseating portrayal of the lonely haunts of the junkie and homosexual in New York City, a new Negro writer, Charles Wright, curses the miscegenation that made him a "minority within a minority":

> "Born . . . half and half. . . . I am tan, a yellowish-brown. . . . Beige. I am a man of color. La Ronde began after my ancestors sailed in

[14] *Ibid.,* p. 69. [15] *Ibid.,* pp. 143, 144.

> from Africa. . . . I wish them many seasons in a syphilitic hell. . . . They make me an outsider. . . . They called me dago as a child, before my curls turned to kinks. . . . I am the result of generations of bastard Anglo-Saxon, African, Blackcreek, and Choctaw Indian blood."[16]

In this motley tale of sexual perversion and human depravity "sleek-haired Mexican boys with loud sport shirts" wait for rich women to pick them up and drive them to their palatial residences "paying for what they couldn't get free at home." A Negro blues singer gets into "a mess with a white man in Kansas City." The narrator is accosted in a bar by a fashionably dressed but frustrated white woman who conveys him in "her big Chrysler" to an elegant stone ranch house. When she cringes before his advances he remarks hatefully:

> "Look at me, white woman. Look at what you want and what you don't want. I know you'd pass me like the plague on the street. I know my looks got me through that front door. Otherwise back door, Boy! . . ."

Finally he "held her gently" in his arms and "stroked her silver hair until she went to sleep."[17]

Robert Gover's *One Hundred Dollar Misunderstanding,* hailed by reviewers as an exceptional first novel "in the tradition of Huck Finn and Holden Caulfield" tells of a white college boy's weekend escapade with a teenage colored prostitute in which "a series of miscalculations" lead to a '"hilariously funny" but "singeing commentary on life." Sex and race are profusely intermingled in this attempt at bawdy comedy. Fraternity buddies chatter about the "sexual superiority" of Negroes. Although white men can satisfy their biological urges in the Negro red light district, they would be

[16] Charles Wright, *The Messenger* (New York: Crest, 1964), p. 85. Used by permission of Farrar, Straus and Company.

[17] *Ibid.,* pp. 41 ,42, 50, 51.

appalled at the thought of having a Negro girl friend or wife. The imaginary leading character in the book is abashed at the possibility of being seen in any public place with a Negro woman:

> "I'm not a Segregationist by any means. But . . . they have their places and we have ours. To eat at, I mean. . . . I could just see myself walking into an all-colored place . . . with her, and with all those evil-looking Negroes just standing there doing nothing, staring at us . . . ."[18]

Throughout the narrative, the whiteness of her male companion is constantly injected into the musings of the Negro prostitute:

> "I say 't myself . . . Girl now you got you a sweet Whiteboy loverman, maybe he kin teach you bout . . . how come the Russianfolks an them Whitefolks wanna blow each others up . . . Whiteboy. So much you don know, it ain even funny. . . . I say, Man I ain pritty. I'm *black!* . . ."[19]

Thus, novel after novel underscores the coexistence of color prejudice and interracial sexual vice. Fiction, as well as undeniable facts, should remind Christians that sex relations between the races is not an issue so delicate that the church can afford to remain silent. Wide publicity was given to the marriage between Sammy Davis, Jr., Negro entertainer, and blonde Swedish actress, May Britt. Eartha Kitt, Negro singer, married the white son of a Los Angeles real estate investor. Miss Kitt was quoted as saying that her mother-in-law referred to her as "my little suntanned daughter."

Once again demagogues in the South could conjure up the specter of miscegenation when they discovered that Charlayne Hunter, the first Negro girl to attend the University of Georgia, had secretly been married to a white classmate from a prominent "well-bred" family. "It is the end of the world," was the melancholy ejacula-

[18] Robert Gover, *One Hundred Dollar Misunderstanding* (New York: Ballantine, 1963), pp. 160-61. Used by permission of Grove Press, Inc.

[19] *Ibid.,* pp. 98, 152, 168.

tion ascribed to the bridegroom's father when the secret leaked out. Georgia politicians called the marriage "a shame and a disgrace," while the State Attorney General warned that the couple would be subject to prosecution if they dared to reappear in their home communities.[20]

For anyone who believes that there is such a thing as "racial purity," or that God decreed the permanent segregation of the races, such developments must appear as catastrophic and blasphemous. Authoritative information from the perspective of both science and theology needs to be disseminated to counteract wild rumors and misleading half-truths which appeal to pride and prejudice.

As the Negro drive for equality spread across the country during the centennial observance of the Emancipation Proclamation scandalmongers whispered that marriages between Negroes and whites were becoming more common. *U. S. News and World Report* interviewed "leading authorities" to get at the "facts." Dr. Gunnar Myrdal, Swedish social economist, whose 1944 study on "the Negro Problem and Modern Democracy"[21] was credited with influencing the 1954 ruling of the Supreme Court, pointed out that Negroes are not eager to marry whites. What they resent as an "open rebuff" to their dignity is the forcible interposition of a law which makes it a crime for them to cross the line in marital relations. Intermarriage is a nightmare for uneasy whites; it is not the center of Negro concern. Oddly enough, what is lowest on the Negro scale of values ("social equality") is what white Americans dread the most. Fair employment practices, decent housing, and equal educational opportunities are at the top of the Negro's list of demands, not bed partnerships with white women.

The Negro president of Howard University, Dr. James M. Nabrit, Jr., doubts that racial intermarriage will increase rapidly during the years ahead and suggests that it would only compound the difficulties of the Negro. That we can speak of a superior race is

[20] Cf. *Newsweek* (September 16, 1963), pp. 27, 28.

[21] Gunnar Myrdal, *An American Dilemma* (New York: Harper, 1944).

flatly denied by Dr. W. Montague Cobb, an anatomist and physical anthropologist who has made biological studies of the U. S. Negro. Dr. Margaret Mead, ethnologist and professor at Columbia University, poignantly observes that we already have a blending of races in our country. The result of integration might be "a decreasing amount of illegal intermixture." When Negro women are equally protected with white women, "interbreeding" would be supplanted by intermarriage; but in all likelihood there would be less interracial sex activity than there was formerly under slavery or during the days when Negro women had no redress against the assaults of white men.[22]

Just how prevalent is racial intermarriage? No one really knows. There are no official statistics to show how many Negroes are married to whites. Estimates do not agree. "A 1956 survey indicated that in states where mixed marriages are legal, fewer than 1 in 20 married Negroes have non-Negro spouses and fewer than 1 in 200 of all marriages are between white and Negro." A New York lawyer who investigated miscegenation laws estimated that "there are almost one million interracial married couples in the U. S." Of this number, he surmises that "some 810,000 . . . are not known as mixed marriages because they involve persons of mixed ancestry 'passing' as whites."[23]

In 1960 the Church of England published a 51-page pamphlet, written by eight clergy and laymen, in which they urge Anglicans to welcome colored people into the churches, act firmly against discriminatory practices, and exercise sane judgment in view of the prospect of interracial marriage. "The whole purpose of God in the creation and redemption," says the study, "is to create one family. . . ." Moreover, "it is our considered view that there is no essential difference between marriages contracted between persons

[22] Cf. *U. S. News and World Report,* LV (November 18, 1963), pp. 84-93. A dissenting view is expressed by Dr. Henry E. Garrett, a professor of psychology for 33 years at Columbia University, who claims that "racial mixing could be catastrophic" because the Negro is deficient in "abstract intelligence!"

[23] *Ibid.,* p. 87.

of the same 'race' and interracial marriages. . . . If the local parish sees the marriage of two of its members in this light, it can make all the difference to the relationship which that marriage will develop to the community at large, by showing that the bond which binds Christians together is stronger than the color bar which separates them."

My own response to the arguments of segregationists and the fears related to racial intermarriage have perhaps been summarized best in a letter which I wrote in September, 1959 to a Mr. M—— in Fort Worth, Texas, who was upset over a news report appearing in *The Lutheran Layman* about essays that I had delivered at the Human Relations Workshop at Valparaiso University. To have interracial sex relations blessed by the rituals and prayers of the church, he protested, would be to validate unnatural lust. He construed as Social Gospel, if not communism, my assertion that "the Lutheran church cannot expect many Negro followers until it has demonstrated a sincere interest in helping the Negro acquire his social and political rights." He accused me of using the promise of sexual liberty to entice Negroes away from their own churches. And to clinch his refutation of my position he enclosed two newspaper clippings about Negroes and whites arrested for sexual debauchery.

My answer included the following: "Dear Mr. M—— . . . It is obvious that you have completely misunderstood the import of what I have written concerning racial intermarriage and sex relations. I have not advocated 'mixed' marriages to accelerate the rate of integration in our churches. I have not suggested that Christians marry a person of another color to prove that they are free of racial bias or to set an example for the rest of the community. In unmistakable language I have declared that 'in view of the social repercussions and the heartache that must ensue, only the foolhardy would recommend that people deliberately cross the color line to seek their marriage partners. . . .'

"At the same time I stressed that there are no biological or moral reasons why interracial marriage should be prohibited. Only the vulgar and ignorant can continue to speak of 'mongrelization' as though marriage between Negroes and whites is a sin against God and nature. Nowhere do the Scriptures of the Old or New Testament intimate that marriage is to be avoided between certain segments of the human family. All humanity, of every shade of color, and with an infinite variety of physical characteristics, has been created by God. All are His children. All are potential heirs of salvation in Christ. Certainly Christians should not uphold artificial barriers that God has neither commanded nor intended. 'The selection of a husband or a wife,' I wrote, 'is after all a decision left to personal preference.' Quoting Hebrews 13:4 I recalled that 'marriage is honorable in all, and the bed undefiled; but whoremongers and adulterers God will judge.'

"Marriage between black and white, if entered into voluntarily with the same honorable intentions that are assumed in any marriage between two avowed Christians, is not to be frowned upon as something unclean or improper, but is to be 'blessed by the ritual and prayers of the Church. And after they are married the Church should endeavor to dissuade its members from treating them any differently than other *bona fide* members of the Body of Christ.'

"The news items which you enclosed, Mr. M——, 'Platters Spun into Court to Sing on Morals Charge' and 'Three Negroes Get Death Sentence'—fall into another category. These affairs are not God-approved sex relations or blessed matrimony. Rape, prostitution, and illicit sexual liaisons come under the condemnation of the same God who sanctions and encourages marriage according to His created order. Contrary to the implications of your appended notes I most assuredly do not think that the Lutheran Church should 'bless' the Platters or their female companions for violating the laws of God and man. If the Negroes convicted of raping two white women in Georgia are really guilty I believe they deserve to be punished.

"However, Christians should insist that equal justice and equal rights be granted to all of our citizens. We might well wonder if the death penalty is not too severe for some rape cases. There is always the question whether or not the person assaulted is entirely innocent. Then, too, how many white men in the South have been sent to the electric chair for sexually exploiting Negro women? Have you considered how the non-marriage laws of Georgia and other states are economically and socially discriminatory in that they specifically deny to the Negro woman and her offspring the same safeguards from abuse with which the members of the white race are abundantly surrounded? You did not mention the rape of a Negro Florida coed by white men. Was this act any less contemptible and ignoble than the violation of a white woman by a Negro man? The Bible knows no distinction. And, if Christians contend for preserving traditions and laws which trample on the human dignity of 'the least of these My brethren' they are grieving the Head of the Church.

"In some areas like Brazil or Hawaii, the social penalties for crossing the color line in marriage are not so severe. When I plead for more Christian sympathy and understanding in regard to racial intermarriage I am thinking of the thoughtless cruelty of some people who, by their derogatory remarks and malicious acts, tend to embitter the lives of the partners in such a marriage. I am disturbed by the plight of German girls who married Negro GI's, and through no fault of their own, are confined to the urban ghettoes in which minorities are compelled to live. I have in mind the perpetual heartache and untold unhappiness of parents and children who suffer needlessly because of irrational prejudices. And I am ashamed when I observe that professed Christians share in and augment these baneful attitudes by their unyielding opposition to that which God does not disapprove.

"No, I do not urge that we 'proselyte' Negroes away from their own churches and Negro pastors 'with the debasing enticement of interracial sex relations.' At the same time I sincerely believe that the worshiper should have the freedom to attend any Christian

Church of his choice and to affiliate with a 'white church' if he so desires, especially when it is located in the same community where he lives. Under no circumstances dare we draw a color line at the entrance to our churches, at the communion rail, or even at our social gatherings. Christian love knows no bounds and must surmount and overcome the sinful divisions imposed upon us by our segregated society. If all Christians, Negroes and whites, are joined together in the perfect unity of the Body of Christ, we cannot project all expression of that unity to some invisible realm, nor fail to demonstrate our love for one another in Christ already now. For 'he who does not love his brother whom he has seen, cannot love God whom he has not seen.' (I John 4:30*b*). And how can we exhibit our oneness in Christ if we live at a distance from one another, if we preserve our segregated churches, if we do not worship and work together?"[24]

[24] Cf. Moellering, *op. cit.,* pp. 20, 21, 27, 29.

9 The Call to Effective Social Action: The Response of the Christian Conscience

Before the Christian conscience can be aroused to participate in constructive measures designed to insure social justice, it will have to be disabused of misapprehensions that have been used to postpone action or avoid responsibility. There are certain theological stumbling blocks which must be removed.

The residue of doctrinal distortion and misunderstanding inherited from the age of slavery still confuses people within, and outside of, the "Bible belt."

One example is the belief that the origin of the Negro race can be traced to the curse of Ham. This story is still being peddled in some neighborhoods where racism thrives. Taylor Caldwell revived the legend in her novel *Dear and Glorious Physician.*[1] A few years back *Christianity Today* printed a letter from a prominent preacher in Dallas, Texas, which included the affirmation:

> . . . we do believe that God's Word teaches, that the Lord Himself assigned the Canaanites, the servile division of the Hamitic, or Negro race a place of servitude, not slavery (cf. Genesis 9 and Joshua 9).

[1] Taylor Caldwell, *Dear and Glorious Physician* (New York: Doubleday, 1959).

> And woe to any white man who tries to take the Negroes out of the place where God put them.[2]

Few biblical scholars today treat the early portions of Genesis as sober history to be taken in a literal sense; but even if this were done, it would not yield the results which white supremacists have intended. Everett Tilson has shown that "at least five assumptions underlie the use of this text [Gen. 9:22-25] in support of segregation." To make the argument valid it would have to be established:

> (1) that God pronounced the curse; (2) that the curse be biologically transferable; (3) that Ham be the original victim of the curse; (4) that the children of the original victim of the curse be slaves; (5) that the original victim of the curse be a member of the Negroid race.[3]

Exegetically and archeologically these assumptions have been tested and found untenable.[4] Only sheer obscurantism and obstinacy can keep them alive.

A study of the Old Testament prophets must convince us that the search for an enlightened social conscience in the name of God did not start with the twentieth century. Twenty-eight hundred years ago the worship of God apart from true morality was detested as a sham and an abomination. Jesus thought it appropriate to quote Hosea, "I desire steadfast love and not sacrifice," as a refutation of his critics. The Book of Isaiah begins with a description of the disasters which had befallen Israel, and the impassioned complaint of the prophet renounces the means which have been used to appease the Lord. The sacrifice of animals, the burning of fat, and

[2] *Christianity Today* (March 2, 1959), p. 24.

[3] Everett Tilson, *Segregation and the Bible* (Nashville: Abingdon, 1958), p. 23.

[4] Cf. J. Ernest Shufelt, "Noah's Curse and Blessing, Genesis 9:18-27," *Concordia Theological Monthly*, XVII (October, 1946), pp. 737-41; cf. A. H. Sayce, *The Races of the Old Testament* (Oxford, England: Religious Tract Society, 1891).

the clouds of incense were futile. What God wanted was a holy life and the righting of social wrongs. "Your hands are full of blood," is his accusation. He pleads: "Wash yourselves; make yourselves clean; remove the evil of your doings from before my eyes; cease to do evil, learn to do good; seek justice, correct oppression; defend the fatherless; plead for the widow" (Isa. 1:15*b*-17).

While the church as an institution has often been identified with the ruling classes, the sympathy of the prophets was expressed for the poor and dispossessed. Sharp invectives were hurled against the greedy aristocracy who "join house to house, who add field to field" (Isa. 5:8) until a country of sturdy peasants is turned into a domain of gigantic estates. Severe woes were called down upon the ruthless "capitalists" who "sell the righteous for silver, and the needy for a pair of shoes" (Amos 2:6), and against the venality of the judges who took bribes and had a double standard of law, one for the wealthy and another for the poor.

Too often during the nineteenth century, and even today, the Christian church has been, and continues to be, the exponent of bourgeois respectability. Too readily it has salved the conscience of the dominant economic group which has offered it protection and financial support. The suppression of a large racial minority has been condoned, if not actually defended. The struggle of the laboring class was long viewed with suspicion. The Marxian critique of the church, although exaggerated, has not been altogether inaccurate. The clergy in western Europe and the United States, on the whole, have reflected a middle-class viewpoint, and have fostered a type of church life which appeals to the bourgeoisie. The people in the inner city have been abandoned by the congregations which have sold their property and moved to the suburbs. The plight of the proletarian immigrants has been ignored. The discrimination practiced against the Negro (in some quarters) has been dismissed as a social problem outside the province of the church.

With the prophets it was not so. They were the champions of

the oppressed. They felt that it was one of their chief duties to speak up in behalf of the voiceless masses—to stand up for the rights of the helpless. In the name of their religion they were preachers of righteousness and social reform.

Twentieth-century Christians find it difficult to project themselves into the ancient and medieval periods when slavery was assumed to be ingrained in the natural order of things. "How could Jesus and the apostles remain silent in the face of such an appalling evil?" is the inquiry raised with moral indignation by post-Civil War generations and people contemporary with the clamor for racial equality. The most obvious answer would be that our Lord and his early disciples did not deem it to be their mission to marshal forces for the reconstruction of the social order. Spiritual freedom was offered to all irrespective of personal independence or physical bondage. In Christ all distinctions between Jew and Gentile, male and female, color and clan, were pronounced inconsequential. But the full social implications of such "revolutionary" assertions were not generally perceived until the irresistible pressures of our own day forced them upon our attention. No doubt, Paul and his followers, for the most part, were not interested in any kind of social salvation that would eradicate prevalent injustices. Nor were they optimistic enough to anticipate favorable changes. Human nature was depicted as inescapably sinful and a corrupt world was hastening toward its doom. All the while, however, Christians were also propagating the Good News of God's gracious intervention in human affairs. If men and women by baptism could bury their selfishness and animosities with Christ in his death and join the Resurrected One on a higher plane of living where self-yielding love predominates, then the maltreatment of unfortunate individuals and the exploitation of defenseless groups could not be glossed over with indifference.

The New Testament seemed to be devoid of material that could be used to sensitize and grieve the Christian conscience. Those who profited from slavery, as well as those who were simply adverse to upsetting the social order, would always quote with finality such passages as I Peter 2:18: "Servants, be submissive to your masters with all respect, not only the kind and gentle but also to the overbearing." Such interpreters never failed to note that the writer proceeded to inculcate patience in suffering and held before the hapless slave the example of the Servant of God who "when he was reviled, did not revile in return."

The use of such references (along with parallel verses like Ephesians 6:5, "Slaves, be obedient to those who are your earthly masters, with fear and trembling") has continued to be a regrettable device for deadening the Christian conscience and silencing critics of Negro enslavement. What is forgotten, aside from the human limitations of first-century Christian vision, is the cultural milieu within which this counsel was given. Entrenched as the system was, what could a minority of Christians do to abolish the deplorable relationship of master and slave? There would have been little hope of eliminating the nefarious institution of slavery by a head-on revolution. Given the existing situation, it would have been suicidal to instigate an insurrection. Whenever that method had been tried it had resulted in making the lot of the slaves even more intolerable. However, there might have been a wider and more direct application of Christian moral power to relieve victims of social iniquity.

In the 1960's, with the last vestiges of colonialism disappearing, and with Negro Americans making rapid strides toward first class citizenship, it becomes anachronistic and utterly immoral for "Christian" spokesmen to contend on the basis of Pauline and Petrine texts that compulsory segregation and an inferior status for Negroes is all quite acceptable. At the same time it must be recognized that society has not advanced into some Utopia where controls are no longer necessary and "bosses" have become superfluous. Employees must still take orders from their employers in modern factories and business establishments. The admonitions in I Peter and Ephesians have not become obsolete; they must be recast and reinterpreted for an industrialized-urbanized mode of life in which authoritarian structures and class divisions have arisen which could not be foreseen by Jewish Christians reflecting an agrarian-pastoral background. The needs of our own age may call for more emphasis on an ethic of responsibility and aggressive action than was conceivable when the first Christian documents were penned.

Another doctrinal misunderstanding that has detracted from a sense of Christian responsibility in race relations may be found in expressions about the essence and scope of sin.

The sinfulness of man is a basic assumption and a pervasive theme found in the biblical writings. Already in the book of Genesis we are informed that man is a fallen creature, and consequently it is an invariable rule that "the imagination of man's heart is evil from his youth" (Gen. 8:21). Augustinian and Calvinistic theology has followed St. Paul in affirming the total corruption of our whole human nature:

> Death spread to all men because all men sinned . . . I know that nothing good dwells within me . . . We were by nature children of wrath, like the rest of mankind.[5]

The Augsburg Confession asserts "all men who are propagated according to nature are born in sin. That is to say, they are without fear of God, are without trust in God, and are concupiscent."[6]

The Reformers taught the universality of sin and that it thoroughly saturated human nature so as to make freedom of the will in spiritual matters inconceivable. Luther said that all the specific acts of sin are a result of this radical, innate evil which corrupts man's entire existence. Every sin estranges man from God and breaks off the harmonious relationship for which man was created. In Luther's understanding the essence of sin is unbelief—a rejec-

[5] Rom. 5:12; 7:18; Eph. 2:3.

[6] Article II, *The Book of Concord*, ed. Theodore G. Tappert (Philadelphia: Fortress Press, 1959), p. 29.

tion of God's reconciling love revealed in Christ. From this point of view, sin is not simply isolated deeds or a failure to measure up to a certain standard, but a perverse direction of will, which implies a deviation from the destiny intended for man by God.[7]

Reinhold Niebuhr prefers to discuss sin in terms of human finitude. Man clamors to escape the limitations of his being. Sin is rebellion against God. Only God is Absolute Reality. But throughout his checkered history man has tried to mix the finite with the eternal and claim for himself, his nation, his culture, or his class the center of existence.[8]

Closely related is Paul Ramsey's definition:

> The opposite of all that Christian love means. Any falling short of disinterested love for neighbor for his own sake . . . any falling short of the full definition of obligation contained in I Corinthians 13—this is what is meant when Christians speak of man as sinful. . . . Sin means: anxious self-centeredness or self-centered anxiety.[9]

Kyle Haselden, in his Rauschenbusch lectures of 1959, uses the orthodox concept of original sin to clarify the real nature of prejudice and demonstrate the superficiality of many modern interpretations. The Marxist seeks to explain racial prejudice solely as a rationale for exploitation and is confident that an equal distribu-

[7] Cf. Gustav Aulén, *The Faith of the Christian Church* (Philadelphia: Muhlenberg, 1948), pp. 259, 260.

[8] Reinhold Niebuhr, *An Interpretation of Christian Ethics* (New York: Harper, 1935), p. 81. Cf. Arnold Toynbee, *A Historian's View of Religion* (New York: Oxford University Press, 1956), pp. 3, 5: ". . . Every living creature is striving to make itself into a centre of the Universe. . . . Self-centredness is an intellectual error because no living creature is in truth the centre of the Universe; and it is also a moral error, because no living creature has a right to act as if he were the centre of the Universe. . . ."

[9] Paul Ramsey, *Basic Christian Ethics* (New York: Charles Scribner's, 1950), pp. 290, 291. Cf. Soren Kierkegaard, *The Sickness unto Death* (Princeton: Princeton University Press, 1941), p. 78. Sin is the idolatry of subconscious egotism: the "despair at not willing to be oneself, the despair of weakness"; and "the despair of willing despairingly to be oneself—defiance."

tion of material wealth among all people would prevent class strife and racial conflict. Many psychologists speak in terms of the frustration-aggression hypothesis. Sociologists, correctly affirming that no one is born with race prejudice, go on to make the erroneous assumption of John Locke that the newborn child is a *tabula rasa* upon which the "sensations" of his environment make their imprint. In Pascal's phrase they claim that human nature is "sound, needing no redeemer." In opposition to these theories of social scientists that prejudice in human beings is not inherent but acquired, Haselden asserts that "self-centeredness is the essence of all sin and that prejudice is a specific expression of that sin." Prejudice is a deeper affliction than is understood by our liberal culture. "The secrets of race prejudice, being internal, do not reveal themselves through sociological data, and prejudice in its aboriginal form is impervious to all sociological techniques."[10]

Why then do little children in interracial settings show no awareness of color distinctions? The explanation, Haselden suggests, is simple. "*Racial* hostility in children is not a primary instinct, but undifferentiated hostility," an antagonistic reaction toward whatever thwarts self-will, "is a primary instinct." Racial prejudice, religious bigotry, social snobbery are acquired traits, but they can only be learned because of man's inherent pride and selfishness. Even in Brazil and Hawaii, where the races intermingle quite freely, there are class distinctions and various forms of social tension. Every "in-group," Haselden argues, has always had an "out-group." Racial prejudice is not an unprecedented phenomenon, "but simply the latest and most virulent form of man's ancient urge for self-exaltation." From a historical perspective we recognize that:

> The Jew had his gentile; the Greek had his barbarian; the Roman had his non-Roman; the crusaders had their infidel; the fifteenth-

[10] Kyle Haselden, *The Racial Problem in Christian Perspective* (New York: Harper, 1959), pp. 77, 78.

century Roman Catholics had their heathens; the English had their Irish; the Lutherans had their Anabaptists; the Nazis had their non-Aryans; and now the white man has his Negro.[11]

Stripped of their race prejudices, racists would become emotionally insecure. Prejudice is like alcohol for the alcoholic. It is an indispensable narcotic that kills the pain of disappointment and the ache of inferiority. Or it assuages the guilty conscience of the exploiter who gains his wealth and power at the expense of another race and boasts of his actions in pointing to his natural superiority.

No sociological remedy, no psychiatric treatment can probe to the root of this problem. Every sin is ultimately a sin against God, and Christianity alone has the solution. Only a complete renovation of man's whole being can eradicate sinful prejudice. Only an encounter with the living God, only the experience of divine forgiveness in the redemptive power of the cross can cause a man to see all other men on an equal plane with himself as fellow creatures, common sinners, and co-heirs of an eternal destiny. Realistic in its appraisal of human nature, Christian theology at its best is not inordinately pessimistic. "Man," says Haselden, "is not an immutable substance upon which heredity has set an unbreakable seal, nor is he a plastic which flows helplessly into whatever molds environment provides."[12] As a new creation of God's Spirit, with the love of Christ dwelling in him, the regenerate man can be absolved of arrogance and bigotry.

Thus Christian anthropology helps us understand the true nature of racial prejudice, and Christian soteriology expounds the most potent means for its extermination.

Even so, it is a one-sided emphasis which restricts sin to the guilt

[11] *Ibid.*, pp. 80-83.

[12] *Ibid.*, p. 87.

of the individual. Classical and modern theology, through its most penetrating thinkers, has often had a profound insight into the dimension of evil and the incurable perversity of human nature. The major deficiency in the traditional definitions of sin has undoubtedly been the failure to detect its corporate character and denounce its appearance within social institutions. Not only among mystics and spiritualists has the alienation of the individual from God been stressed to the exclusion of concern for the manifestations of evil emanating from an immoral society. Many Christians have presumed that individual salvation (forgiveness of sins and restoration of fellowship with God) can be attained and preserved intact as an individual possession, without any urge to contribute to the "redemption" of society as a whole from the ills which beset it.

Even worse, and what has contributed most to the failure of the organized churches to alleviate social distress, has been the pietistic and moralizing tendency. Much of Protestantism has bypassed the more profound definitions of sin as unbelief, alienation, or egocentricity, and has concentrated on a denunciation of individual infractions of the law. Personal vices, crime, and sensuality have been viewed as the most serious violations of God's will. Reverting to the nominalistic position, many Pietists and Puritans have intimated that if one can avoid individual transgressions of what is right and proper, then one has almost ceased to sin. With this kind of legalistic approach, it is suggested that one become holy by refraining from certain prohibited acts and scrupulously observing a moralistic code. Sin is often thought of in terms of "bad habits" like smoking, drinking, or card playing. Lust and sexual aberrations are usually at the head of the list as cardinal sins. Revivalistic preaching in America has generally fulminated against these sins of the flesh. Repentance has implied a willingness to become "respectable" and avoid acts which are disapproved by "nice" people. There have been elements in the preaching of Billy Graham which strongly emphasize this interpretation of sin. The prohibition crusade was based upon the assumption that alcoholic beverages were the root of all evil and might be outlawed by legislative edict. A kind of "bourgeois" morality becomes the norm by which the distinction between saints and sinners can be detected.

However, sin is not just a private transaction between the sinner and God. It is a rebellion against God which results not only in the disturbance of the individual but also in the turbulent upheavals of society. The full gravity of our sinful state is not understood until we perceive that we are all enmeshed in the large-scale sins of devastating wars and economic and racial discrimination.

The social dimension of sin must not be overlooked or underestimated. Even after we have overcome our own personal prejudices and have avoided overt acts of violence or any unfriendly gestures directed against people of another color, it does not mean that we have discharged our full responsibility in race relations. We are still "caught up" in the sins of our society which magnify racial arrogance and economic injustice.

The Christian doctrine of original sin must be applied not only to the biological inheritance of a corrupt humanity but also to what Walter Rauschenbusch called the social transmission of sin. Not only are we born *with* a depraved nature, but we are born *into* a sin-saturated community. The mistake of some advocates of the Social Gospel was to stress the latter to the exclusion of the former.

In our present-day illustrations of the dominion of darkness we must not confine ourselves to personal faults or sins of sensuality. We are all, Christians included, implicated in the sins of our immoral society. Racketeering among labor leaders, the bribery of government officials, and unfair employment practices, are all symptoms of the disease that permeates our whole political and economic structure. We do not escape these evils, we do not protect our innocence, solely by preserving a high level of virtue in our own private life. Entering into illegal housing covenants or profiting from investments in slum housing are only a few of the many ways in which churchgoing people are implicated in the collective guilt of the economy and the society in which they live. Failing to stand up and defend what is true and right and honorable is their sin of omission.[13]

> Blest be the tie that binds
> Our hearts in Christian love;
> The Fellowship of kindred minds
> Is like to that above.

So congregations sing in the words of a popular, if somewhat sentimental, hymn. Every time that people confess their faith in the words of the Apostles' Creed—and in many localities this means almost every occasion for public worship—they piously express their belief in: "The Holy Christian Church, the Communion of Saints."

It was our Lord's intention that the communion of saints should be more than a "spiritual" relationship. Full unity in Christ demands that we have a vital concern for the total welfare—physical, spiritual, psychological, social, economic, and political—of our brothers and sisters. People who are moved by the same energizing Spirit of God, people who eat and drink of the same Body and Blood provided by the one Savior to whom they profess a common allegiance—these people cannot remain indifferent to the needs and difficulties faced by fellow Christians. If one member of the Body of Christ is suffering, the other members cannot be anaesthetized against the pain. "For each other flows the sympathizing tear."

What does this creedal affirmation of faith in the communion of saints imply for the relation that should exist between newly organized congregations in the thriving suburbs, long established congregations in the more stable parts of the city, and the churches undergoing a sociological transformation in the inner city? The eye cannot say to the ear "I have no need of you." The leg and the arm are attached to the same body and contribute to the unity and harmonious operation of the whole organism. The employer who belongs to the church cannot refuse to dine with his employees

[13] Cf. James 4:17: "Whoever knows what is right to do and fails to do it, for him it is sin."

who profess the same faith. The college professor cannot scorn conversation with an illiterate fellow member of the congregation. The suburbanite cannot ignore the existence of his brother in Christ who lives in an overcrowded tenement district. The Caucasian Christian cannot wish to avoid all religious and social contacts with the Negro who acknowledges the same Lord.

As recently as a decade or so ago the Protestant churches in our large metropolitan centers in the downtown districts or in areas experiencing sudden population changes were abandoning their original sites without stirring up so much as a ripple of protest. For a church to sell its property, relocate, and follow its members to a more attractive suburban environment was regarded as a normal and unavoidable procedure.

Within the last five years or so the number of churches "threatened" by the invasion of unfamiliar "aliens" has risen to such an alarming number that church leaders have been shocked into a reappraisal of what is transpiring. The sale of valuable property at almost giveaway prices may have helped induce a little more thinking about the problem. The steady trek to the "greener pastures" has sometimes resulted in an unnecessary duplication of facilities for worship and parish education within the same denomination.

At least some consciences have been bothered by the fact that where there are multitudes of people huddled together in the inner city and where human needs and physical misery are most evident, there are few, if any, Protestant churches remaining on the scene. Thus it has happened that many conferences have been held to discuss the plight of the urban church in transition and most major denominations have passed resolutions encouraging their mission boards to help counteract the "flight from blight." For some time now we have thoroughly lamented the demise of churches in the inner city and we have promised God and our church conventions to do better.

But do our churchmen really understand the baffling problems confronting the church which seeks to preserve a useful ministry in an unstable neighborhood? Are we planning realistically and effectively to undergird and sustain the efforts of these churches? Are we properly applying the doctrine of the communion of saints to the inner city?

What can be done to remove the barriers between suburban Christians and their brethren in the inner city? What steps might be taken to make the entire metropolitan area more conscious of its unity in Christ? How ought this unity to manifest itself in reciprocal relations? How can we demonstrate that the bond of Christian love is such a unifying factor that it must overcome the divisive features of our society? How can we relate people of diverse cultural backgrounds and different educational levels with one another?

Surrounded by a constantly flowing population, an inner city church is likely to be unstable and insecure. The role it is destined to play in building the kingdom of God may be compared to that of a receiving station which makes the initial contacts; introduces new people, during the few months or years that they are in the vicinity, to the way that leads to eternal life; and then seeks to have the good work which was begun in them advanced to a deeper stage of Christian knowledge and understanding by another church in the neighborhood to which they move. Or a church trying to reach such a mobile population may find itself serving as a fueling station which supplies the means of grace and offers counsel and aid mostly to temporary residents and guest members. Someone has said that ministering to people in deteriorating parts of the city or in public housing projects is like trying to reach a passing parade. You can hear the sound of many feet marching by. But what will this passing parade of people do to help a minister build up a congregational organization, and what is he to do for assistance and resources if eventually he finds himself with no organizational backing left at all?

The inner-city church needs a strong solid core of members who can give it some continuity and sense of permanency. The financial and administrative problems loom high and can become utterly disheartening in a church which must work among the lowest income groups and which has a rapid turnover of membership. When the financial and administrative burden becomes overwhelming, and there are only a few dependable stalwarts left to shoulder the load, morale suffers and disintegration is accelerated rather than halted. It does not require a prophet to perceive that such a church may soon be on the verge of total dissolution.

Subsidy from mission treasuries may be unavoidable. But this is only part of the answer, and perhaps not the main part. To turn apparent defeat into glorious victory the New Testament vision of the communion of saints needs to be translated from a cloudy abstraction into a vivid and meaningful demonstration of the way Christian love can be effectively applied in a modern industrialized society. To alleviate the distress, more is needed than words of sympathy or contributions of money, useful and desirable as these tokens of concern may be. Christians must be found who have "presented their bodies as a living sacrifice to the Lord" and are willing to give up personal convenience in their local churches where their membership and help is not indispensable to answer a higher call to more urgent duty and directly affiliate themselves with the declining, and sometimes despondent, churches in our changing communities.

The superhighways and expressways completed or under construction in our large cities have made this "rescue operation" increasingly practical. Hitherto we have assumed that Christians moving out of the old neighborhoods should be encouraged to join the church closest to their new home as promptly as possible. For most people this will probably continue to be an advisable procedure. To avoid backsliding and loss of interest they need the stimulus of a pastor and church home near at hand. But surely we have other Christians who are more firmly rooted in their convictions, and who possess a mission zeal that could be used to the greatest advantage by involving them in activity where the challenges are the greatest —especially where the unsettled newcomers to the city are groping in spiritual darkness and desperately need the hope that can be provided only by the gospel of Christ.

Have we possibly made a serious miscalculation in concentrating most of our missionaries and funds for investment in prosperous suburbs? Probably not if we are thinking only of establishing as many new self-supporting congregations as rapidly as we can with a minimum of financial risk. But what conclusions might we draw if we think more in terms of the parable of the Great Supper with the Master sending his emissaries to the highways and byways? Or if we ask ourselves how much we are accomplishing in patterning our ministry after that of Jesus who laid so much stress on reaching the down-trodden and despised classes of society and brought mercy and healing to people who were overlooked by the "official church"? Could there be some truth to the charge, made by one layman at a church convention, that our prevailing mission policy tends to reward those who have shirked their responsibilities and deserted the Christian cause where the "going was too rough"? What he meant was that people who abandon the older churches leave them to struggle with their manifold difficulties while they retreat to a new suburb where the mission board hastens to grant them a substantial loan or gift for building a new church.

In all this have we not disregarded the New Testament concept of the communion of saints? We would recommend that mission directors confer with suburban and inner city parish pastors to devise a workable plan by which "expendable" volunteers can be transferred to "dying" congregations to bolster morale and serve as lay evangelists, lay teachers, and business managers. We venture to predict that the adoption of this policy could mark a turning point in the history of urban Christianity and that the missionary challenge and personal involvement and interaction between inner city and suburbs would result in a spiritual upsurge in whole metropolitan areas.

This bold suggestion requires more clarification. It should be understood that only those congregations which have adopted an all-inclusive mission policy and seriously intend to grapple with the problems of a multifarious population and foster a vital ministry will be eligible for this "shot in the arm" treatment. No congregation should be permitted to take advantage of this offer simply because it wants to preserve the traditions of its forefathers a little longer.

Further, it should be spelled out in unmistakable terms that the importation of willing and trained laymen from other congregations should never be used to deprive a local resident or a new convert of an opportunity for service, or in any way retard the development of the stewardship and talents and money in the subsidized congregation. To whatever degree is possible, even in the most transient and insecure congregation, the full utilization of available resources in manpower and funds should be encouraged.

We might add the supplementary suggestion that to insure financial security a "patron membership plan" could be introduced. This might consist in drawing up a list of former members and interested people who have expressed a concern about the future destiny of the congregation in the inner city, but who for valid reasons are unable to participate directly. They would gladly contribute ten, twenty, or more dollars a year (without reducing their pledge to their home church) to help pay the salary of a missionary, deaconess, or parish worker. All those who become patron members should then be invited to make periodic visits to the church which they are supporting. Let them see by firsthand observation what their contributions are achieving. Keep them informed with occasional mailings of a news bulletin prepared especially for their consumption. Make them feel that they have a kind of secondary membership in the inner city which does not need to interfere with the obligations which they have assumed in their local congregations.

A visitation program might be introduced by which representatives from outlying congregations would be encouraged to attend worship services occasionally, observe Sunday school, and share in some of the parish activities with people who would otherwise be unknown to them. Outlying congregations, in turn, might invite delegations from the inner city churches to worship with them on special occasions. A Ladies Aid society in a suburban community might plan a program to which it specifically invites the Altar Guild from the downtown church. Youth Leagues might sponsor joint meetings to promote better understanding between Negro and white teenagers.

Philip Johnson, who integrated a white congregation in Chicago in the early 1950's and is now director of public relations for the National Lutheran Council, has proposed that strong suburban congregations adopt an inner-city church, arranging to transport groups to church, young people and adults, in a two-way exchange, "not just for one Sunday a year, but on a regular basis." Some churches have more talent than they really need, Dr. Johnson noted. To share with congregations barely able to survive in tough situations, he affirmed, "is part of bearing one another's burdens, and so fulfilling the law of Christ."[14]

Usually the assumption has been that all-inclusive membership implies recruiting Negroes into white congregations. Why not make it a two-way stream and encourage whites to affiliate with Negro churches? Wherever Negroes are present let there be an uninhibited interchange of members and a full sharing of life and resources. Anything less falls short of complete integration.[15] Deploring the fact that white Christians have too long waited for the Negro to take the initiative, the Episcopal Society for Cultural and Racial Unity called upon "all churchmen . . . to witness to the wholeness of the Church on Whitsunday of 1964 and thereafter by transferring from their present parish to one where the members are predominantly of another color."[16]

Through the mediation of a concerned Christian in Iowa about

[14] *The National Lutheran* (March, 1964).

[15] Cf. *Local Action in the Churches on Race,* the Commission of Religion and Race, National Council of Churches of Christ, in the U. S. A.

[16] *The Vanguard* (March-April, 1964).

ten years ago, young boys and girls of the Negro race were invited to spend a week or two on midwestern farms with Christian families. The children were temporarily "adopted" and treated as part of the family circle. Youngsters from the church I served in Chicago were among the first to be included in this venture which has become an annual project of the Lutheran Human Relations Association of America.

This is much more than an act of charity for the underprivileged. The experience is mutually beneficial. Not only do the city dwellers breathe fresh air for a few weeks and learn to milk cows on a rural holiday, but it has proven to be a worthy device for promoting better racial understanding. White parents discover that Negro children have the same basic desires and needs as their own children. The boys and girls rapidly erase the color line and play together without any thought about the physical distinctions which usually divide their elders. It is doubtful that white children who have been exposed to these favorable associations with Negroes will grow up to be advocates of segregation or will speak disparagingly of their darker complexioned brethren. At the same time it can be assumed that the Negro children returning to their homes in the city will retain some pleasant memories of white people and will be less likely to be suspicious of all people representing the majority race. Without ever hearing a theological definition of the *una sancta* these Christian farmers with their urban guests have broken down some of the partitions erected by a sinful society, and quite unconsciously have put the New Testament ideal into practice on at least a limited scale. Could this be the beginning of a broad movement in which Christian farmers in many parts of the country become hosts for hundreds of otherwise forgotten and often neglected children from the inner city? Could this experience become in any way reciprocal? Could children from suburban and rural homes spend some time with Negro families and other minority groups where adequate housing would allow it? Could this proposal be adopted as a positive, church-sponsored step toward relieving racial tensions and cementing ties between city and country?[17]

Inner-city churches in New York City, Detroit, and Chicago are already experimenting with a kind of "domestic peace corps." University graduates or students who are still in college are often more idealistic-minded and ready to bring personal sacrifices than their elders. Why not tap some of this youthful energy and direct it into useful service in the problem-ridden inner city? Many of the Peace Corps enterprises overseas could be adapted under church auspices for the relief of human misery and an assault on social problems. To meet the crisis in our "city jungles," church boards must be prepared to experiment with new approaches and inaugurate "pilot projects." Experience may demonstrate that our inherited modes of operation are no longer feasible and may have to be radically revised or even discarded entirely.

What can Christians do to help achieve racial harmony and accelerate the achievement of full civic rights for deprived minorities? Basic and preliminary is the eradication of all racial animus in those who are in positions of leadership. Despite protestations to the contrary there is disturbingly abundant evidence that prejudice has not been fully wiped out among our preachers and teachers. Careless remarks, or what may be called concessions to human frailty, obstruct the cleansing power of the gospel. Until our men of the cloth and our educators set an example and give guidance to our people, it should be no wonder that intolerance rears its ugly head among rank and file church members.

More specifically, what proposals can be offered to improve race relations? To whom are we addressing them? In sketching the following suggestions I have in mind the individual Christian, formal and informal associations of Christians, the local congregations, as well as the general body with its responsible executives and boards.

[17] Some of the preceding paragraphs originally appeared as a separate article. See Ralph L. Moellering, "The Inner City and the Communion of Saints," *American Lutheran,* XLII (April, 1959), pp. 7-9, 26.

In some instances the recommendations will pertain more to the individual. Others can be better acted upon by collective units.[18]

1. Churches should redouble efforts to eliminate discriminatory practices in their own midst and demonstrate the ideal of Christian community among their own members. The church should proclaim its message of forgiveness and reclamation in Christ so that through word and sacrament "new beings" are created with new motives. Christians should be constantly reminded that they are to be the "salt of the earth" and the "light of the world." Fully aware of the inescapable reality of evil, they are not to surrender to sin and corruption; instead they should take the lead in constructing a better society in which people will find a more favorable atmosphere for living their Christian convictions. Immediately this implies all-inclusive neighborhood evangelism and membership unrestricted by any racial barriers. Especially in their chosen vocation laymen should be encouraged to make their influence felt in remedying the racial ills that beset us. Imagine what this would mean for lawyers, politicians, industrialists, and real estate owners! If the churches would answer the criticism of the secularists who scornfully say, "Physician heal thyself," they must act promptly and decisively to eliminate all traces of segregation from their own institutions. Church-related schools, charities, homes for the aged, youth camps, etc., must announce and prove their readiness to serve all members of their communion without regard for color distinctions. Publishing houses and hospitals must not decline to employ persons from racial and cultural minorities on the same basis of character and ability with which they receive other applicants. Let the church set the pattern with its own fair employment practices!

2. The time is long overdue for us to take steps to discontinue all forms of separate and unequal facilities for Negroes. No one should think any longer in terms of special missions for "colored

[18] These proposals, now somewhat abbreviated and altered, first appeared in an article by the author called "The Christian and Race—What Can Be Done?" *American Lutheran,* XVIII (November, 1960), pp. 16-18, 24, 25.

people." Until or unless the ghettoes of our big cities are broken up and diffused, it may be unavoidable to have churches composed predominantly of Negroes, but any deliberate attempt by white congregations to circumvent their responsibility by starting separate mission stations must be repudiated. More students of high aptitude from racial minorities should be recruited for the ministry and other forms of full-time service in the church . White congregations should be taught to accept Negro workers as servants of the Lord. Boards for world missions should be urged to call some Negro clergy for service overseas, not necessarily in Africa but also in Japan, the Philippines, or Latin America. The qualifications of the individual (mental endowment, linguistic ability, missionary zeal, etc.), not his physical appearance, should be the determining factors in making such selections.

3. Communicant integration in local congregations should be accelerated. No appeal to expediency should be allowed to delay or frustrate the reception of all people into the membership of the church irrespective of racial origin or economic status. The teaching of the New Testament undeniably calls for the erasure of the color line in associations between Christians. Neighborhood evangelism dare not overlook any element of the population in the geographical area it is seeking to cover.

4. From his pulpit, in the classroom, and in discussions with the various organizations in the parish, the minister can plead for a sober evaluation of population changes. The danger of characterizing a whole race according to misleading and faulty stereotypes should be pointed out. The dignity and worth of the individual should be stressed. With painstaking effort the pastor will want to guide his people in making a distinction between a false racial explanation of local social phenomena (e.g., crime, illegitimacy, illiteracy) and a valid approach founded on a recognition of the ordinary causes of social retardation. In daily contacts with people, whether of the church's own jurisdiction or the neighborhood at

large, the leaders of the church should seek to bolster morale by denouncing pessimism and providing a new perspective of what the future can bring if all the groups, oblivious of racial affiliation, work cooperatively toward the common good. No doubt the atmosphere of the inner city provides the Christian with an exceptional challenge to be a leaven for good, helping reverse the trend toward conflict and chaos. Faced with the baffling problems of social disintegration the church is called upon to safeguard the conscience of the community.

5. Refute myths (e.g., miscegenation is a sin punished with congenital disorders) with facts (e.g., anthropology and psychology adduce evidence to disprove the allegation that certain races are inferior). Avoid describing any race or nationality with broad generalizations that are inaccurate and misleading (e.g., the Negro "can't do skilled work," he is "a child, with a child's emotional equipment and dependence"). Object to jokes which depend upon reputed racial eccentricities for their humorous import.

6. When an obvious violation of human rights occurs or when a situation condoning injustice persists, Christians should voice their protests. Silence implies consent or indifference. Elected officials may be responsive to expressions of public opinion. It is a mistake to assume that Christians concerned about the disruptive factors in society are limited to prayer and private admonition. Authorities who are abusing their power must be confronted with the spectacle of indignant citizens joining together to resist corruption. At times it may be desirable for a congregation or a group of Christian citizens to make a direct pronouncement expressing their convictions on a particular issue which involves an infraction of the moral law. This may be one of the ways in which suburban churches that have no "minority problem" can commit themselves to the ideal of a non-segregated church in a non-segregated society.

7. Support legislation, both local and national, outlawing the evils of intolerance. Encourage the political party to which you are

attached to enact into law helpful proposals which may be included in their campaign platforms. Write to your congressman and express your views when crucial bills are being debated in Washington. Appeal to the mayor and the responsible officials in your city to stamp out discriminatory practices. Object when the courts or the police mistreat minorities. Work toward opening up hospitals, libraries, and recreational facilities for the use of all people. To quote from the study of John P. Dean and Alex Rosen: "Desegregation that proceeds by firm and decisive steps backed by the responsible authorities is more readily accepted and taken for granted than a halting desegregation that appears unsure of itself."[19]

8. Help open up equal job opportunities in private industry and government. As it stands now most employing firms continue to discriminate. Even though some Negroes may be included on the pay roll they are usually not given the same opportunity to advance on the basis of their qualifications. White-collar positions may be closed to them, regardless of their merits. During periods of economic recession members of minorities are among the first to lose their jobs, as they are among the last to be hired when prosperity is renewed. The churches can do a great deal to counteract these inequities by enlightening their own members, whether they be employers, employees, or consumers, as to the obligation of Christians to contend for fair employment practices. Employers should be urged to hire and promote their workers on the basis of individual worth and skill, without reference to color. Employees should be encouraged to work cooperatively with people of other races, to set an example by treating them with courtesy and friendliness. Customers should be taught to appreciate good service without giving attention to the color of the hand that waits on them.

9. Our churches should stand behind minorities who are seeking to attain their rights through nonviolent resistance and judicial

[19] John P. Dean and Alex Rosen, *A Manual of Intergroup Relations* (Chicago: University of Chicago Press, 1955), p. 70.

action. By word and deed Christians should undergird those who, receiving their inspiration from the Sermon on the Mount, are practicing self-denial and voluntary suffering in overcoming their enemies. Peaceful demonstrations, even picketing and "sit-ins," may be effective and desirable techniques for breaking down the walls of resistance to racial equality.

10. As it stands today some predominantly Christian communities have few, if any, Negroes, Latin Americans, or Indians residing in their midst, while worthy and energetic members of these minority groups are "bottled up" in overcrowded ghettoes which frustrate ambition and discourage morality. A novel and daring venture might be for Christian congregations to facilitate the dispersion and integration of some of these people by actually finding them jobs and housing, and by their example, leading the way for their acceptance as first class citizens by everyone in their own community. In some respects this proposal might be comparable to the resettlement of European DP's in different parts of America after World War II. Small towns and rural areas in the Mid-West might be "infiltrated" in this manner and make a direct contribution to the alleviation of racial tensions in the country. Here we are thinking especially of families which are struggling to "get ahead," but suffer repeated setbacks due to an adverse environment from which there seems to be no escape because of the penalty of color. Let Christians with a sense of compassion and social justice establish an agency which could evaluate cases of this kind and provide for their removal. This could become the instrumentality through which at least a minimum number of the most intelligent and competent could be granted a new "lease on life."

11. More imaginative, almost revolutionary, changes must be made in our approach to an inner city ministry if we are to evangelize the "proletariat"—the mass of unskilled laborers, the Negroes from the rural South, the new immigrants. If we are to refute the charge of sponsoring only "bourgeois-endorsed" churches and emulate the example of Christ, we will have to make a serious

effort to penetrate the ranks of the "toiling masses," not to mention making provision for the mentally inferior, the illiterates, and the social outcasts. We must begin where the people are. This may imply experiments with new types of non-liturgical worship at store front preaching points with biblical exposition and music on a level with the people being approached. It may suggest the desirability of forming "block clubs" and meeting in homes and apartments for prayer and fellowship. While emotional excesses can be checked, allowance will have to be made for more informality and spontaneous expression. The genius of the confessional-minded churches with heavy ritual may have to be reinterpreted through different religious forms. In some situations, depending upon local conditions, it might be advantageous to use a "staff ministry" and include the services of a social worker and perhaps a psychiatrist. Where health and income are sub-standard a clinic might be introduced, served by Christian doctors and medical personnel who indicate their willingness to donate a half day a week or so to such a charitable endeavor. Other possibilities might include a plan for clothing distribution among the destitute, a kind of "soup kitchen" for the hungry, and a carefully screened system for extending small money loans to cover emergencies where people are not eligible for assistance from existing agencies.

12. An amendment or by-law should be added to every congregation's constitution calling for the formation of a Board for Social Action. The function of this board should be to gather information and to study such questions as right to work laws, organized crime, and racial discrimination. Where facts are uncovered which are relevant to Christian concerns, they should be presented to give intelligent guidance to members and help them form their opinions. Sometimes the Christian course of action will be clear and the board can recommend specific measures. Many of the problems will appear ambiguous and several alternatives, none of which can be labelled as the "only Christian solution," may emerge. At least occasionally the congregation may become incensed over a glaring

evil and, through its Board for Social Action, speak with unanimity and persuasiveness. Correspondingly, there should also be a National Board for Social Action composed of theologians who have specialized in social ethics, and lay members who are familiar with problems in labor, industry, and government.[20]

The difficulties involved in gaining decent housing for minorities require special analysis and comment. In most urban centers where the Negro population is rapidly increasing, there is an acute shortage of habitable dwellings. The oldest and most deteriorated housing is usually all that is available for the occupancy of Negro families. The ghettoes into which minority groups have been shunted are filled to overflowing, and the people of darker hue spill over into adjoining neighborhoods where heretofore only Caucasians have been living. The resentments created may flare up into violence. Lives are threatened and race riots may ensue. Some white neighborhoods have tried to exclude Negroes by intimidation or restrictive housing covenants.[21]

It is still argued that if Negroes move into an area, property values will inevitably fall. While it is true that whites sometimes become panic-stricken and quickly sell their homes, thereby undercutting property values, eventually real estate values may return to their earlier level or even rise above it. And the whites who remain have sometimes revised their earlier opinion.

Crucial for the whole proposition of providing housing for racial minorities is equality of opportunity in financing either the building or the purchasing of a new home. The prospective home owner who is a Negro has to hurdle many obstacles in trying to obtain a loan and may be compelled to pay higher rates of interest.[22]

[20] Many denominations and an increasing number of local churches have already made this provision; e.g., the Lutheran Church in America's constitution for congregations includes (Art. X, Sec. 7) a standing committee for social action.

[21] Cf. Herman H. Long, "Housing and Race Relations," *Proceedings*, Lutheran Human Relations Institute (Valparaiso, Ind., 1957), pp. 27-33.

[22] Cf. *An Address to Christians and Churches Concerning Race Relations* (The Church Federation of Greater Chicago, 1957), pp. 8, 9.

Sometimes when Negroes attempt to move into all-white neighborhoods the Caucasian residents profess to be unable to understand why Negroes would not want "to remain with their own people." They accuse the NAACP of stirring up a provocative incident, or they suspect Communist influence. Little do they realize how stifling and depressing it is to be forcibly confined to a congested neighborhood where nearly all available facilities are sub-standard.

Some insight into the predicament of the Negro is shown by John McPartland in his book, *No Down Payment,* which is described on the cover as "an explosive novel of the intimate relationships between young couples in a typical suburban development." In the story Herman Kreitzer, who is a store manager, has employed a Negro, Jim Kemp, as a salesman. Determined that Negroes and Orientals should have "as fair a shake as anybody else" Herman proposed Jim for membership in a luncheon club. Later his Negro employee pays a visit to his residence to inquire about the possibility of obtaining a home in Sunrise Hills—the same area in which he works and represents his store in the service club. Personally, Herman is not adverse to the prospect of having a Negro neighbor, but he is apprehensive about the reaction of the community. He insists that Jim call him by his first name and asks what is wrong with the place where he is now living. Then the Negro he has already befriended explains why he wants to move. It is not that he wants to run away from his own race and be surrounded by white people. As a matter of fact he admits that he would be somewhat ill at ease in a predominantly white residential area. But an all-colored neighborhood usually implies poor schools, lack of recreational facilities, and serious temptations to be faced by his children, such as juvenile gangs, heavy drinking, knifings, and marijuana. To escape from these confinements would be "like getting out into the world after you've been shut up in a kind of open-air prison all your life." Jim tells about his wife who is young and ambitious and wants a chance for a better life. Since he is earning enough money now he does not see why his family should not be entitled to a decent home and better living conditions. Herman listens sympathetically, but he is unwilling to risk his own security by sticking his neck out too far:

> There was no chance of getting a Negro family into Sunrise Hills. He was a practical man and he knew what would happen if he tried to force an issue on it. Betty and the children would suffer. He would be transferred out of the Sunrise Hills store, maybe lose his manager's rating. Jim Kemp would be transferred to the store in the Fillmore district in the city, the one with all-Negro personnel from the manager down. All he had to do to start all that happening was to say one word at the Sunrise Hills development sales office, or say one word to the men at the shopping center, the men Jim Kemp considered as friends.
>
> That was the way it was.
>
> "No, Jim. You can't tell your wife that I might help. I can't."[23]

Up to now the churches have been playing it safe too. Clergymen are often reluctant to antagonize their parishioners by taking a definite stand in favor of desegregated housing. Herman Kreitzer, without the motivation of Christian faith, had at least helped "one Negro across the wall, getting him classified as a salesman instead of porter help." Perhaps he could have done more if the churches in Sunrise Hills had helped guide and shape the sentiments of the community rather than conforming with them. Our Christian convictions about the dignity and worth of all men should not permit us to let discriminatory practices in housing go unchallenged.

What specifically can churches do to improve the situation? They could begin by encouraging their members to study the housing conditions in their own vicinity. Especially where Negroes and whites are living in the same or adjoining communities, committees from their churches could study and work together on the problem. Members who are property owners should be urged to refuse to join restrictive "gentlemen's agreements" or in any way take ad-

[23] John McPartland, *No Down Payment* (New York: Pocket Books, 1957), pp. 159. Reprinted by permission of Simon and Schuster, Inc.

vantage of racial prejudice for their own financial advantage. The churches can act constructively by challenging their people, whether owners or tenants, to remain in an area when its racial composition begins to change, and to cooperate in forming a stabilized neighborhood. A local church can bolster the morale of its members in a depressed section of the city and help stimulate a sense of pride in the whole community.

Property owners, white and Negro alike, should be reproved by their ministers if they are tempted to select tenants on the basis of race. Prophetic voices should be heard from the pulpit, in the press, and through every medium available when greedy real estate operators become wealthy by capitalizing on the fears of white people in a changing area and on the desperate need of Negroes for housing. Real estate dealers in city and suburbs should be made to understand that "the desire of the people in any given neighborhood is to maintain the fine residential qualities of that neighborhood, and should be persuaded that these qualities can be maintained by a careful selection of purchasers regardless of their race, color, creed, or national background."[24]

Church members are often foremost among those opposing new ordinances that would punish discrimination in housing.[25] What is astounding is that they take their stand on "moral grounds" with an almost "righteous indignation" against the proponents of fair housing.

Respectable, churchgoing, middle class, white citizens in Berkeley, California, (the author's home) usually raised two primary objections to the legislation pending there in 1963.[26] The first was

[24] Cf. *An Address to Christians and Churches Concerning Race Relations, op. cit.,* pp. 9, 10. Cf. the advice given by the General Assembly of the Presbyterian Church in the U. S. A. in 1956, namely, that in the sale of residential property Christians should practice non-discrimination.

[25] Much of the material that follows on housing first appeared in an article by the writer, "Freedom and Truth in Housing," *The Cresset* (September, 1963).

[26] The "liberal" city of Berkeley defeated the fair housing ordinance, but the Rumford Law, passed by the state of California in 1963, prohibited racial and religious discrimination in the sale or rental of publicly assisted housing (except duplexes and unoccupied single-family homes) and of privately financed hous-

the claim that private property rights were jeopardized by the stipulation that "it shall be unlawful for the owner of any housing accommodation to refuse to sell, rent or lease or to otherwise deny to or withhold from any person such housing accommodation because of the race, religion, national origin or ancestry of such person." In the estimation of these home owners, insistence upon nondiscrimination in the acceptance of renters or buyers is unwarranted intrusion upon their liberty to utilize or dispose of their property according to their own discretion.

The other troublesome feature of Berkeley's housing ordinance for many self-esteemed Christians was the provision made for enforcement. To put some "teeth" into the measure the notorious "penalty clause" was inserted which declared that "any person who shall in any manner wilfully violate any order of compliance made by the Board (of Intergroup Relations) shall be guilty of a misdemeanor, and upon conviction thereof, shall be punished by a fine not exceeding five hundred dollars or by imprisonment not exceeding six months, or both such fine and imprisonment." Immediately some scaremongers conjured up an image of an upright citizen languishing in prison because a criminally inclined member of a minority group falsely accused him of racial bias in refusing to rent him a room. Many pious Christians instinctively shudder over the use of force under any circumstances and the thought of bolstering fair housing with any form of compulsion utterly repels them.

Both of these major "Christian" objections to the type of housing ordinance proposed for the city of Berkeley and in other American communities need to be examined as to their validity and pertinence.

In the Christian outlook, it should be emphasized, "property rights" are always subordinate to "human rights." One of the most frightful abuses in the history of the Western world, as we have

ing composed of five units or more. No punitive or criminal provisions were included, but half a million California voters signed a petition calling for an initiative constitutional amendment that would revoke California's fair housing law. The amendment passed by a large majority in the November, 1964, election.

already seen, is the way in which biblical material has been distorted to absolutize the economics of capitalism and defend slavery and racial segregation in the name of righteousness.

How insistent is the scriptural record on the "rights of private property"? In the Old Testament concessions are made to the prevailing social relationships, but wealth among the Hebrew people was not regarded as belonging so much to an individual as to a family or the whole community. There was no clearcut division between "private" and "communal" property. To prevent "capitalistic" aggrandizement, safeguards were set up to preserve small shareholders on their ancestral estates. The law of the Sabbatical year proposed that at the end of seven years "every creditor shall release what he has lent his neighbor" (Deut. 15:2). "Thou shalt not steal" was not a commandment introduced to defend the sanctity of private property acquired through dubious means. Its main thrust is against selfishness. No man is to arrogate to himself that which should contribute to the honor and welfare of others.

Christian apologists for "right wing" economics in America today profess to find "proof texts" in the New Testament. "Soak the rich" legislation and "our Marxian graduated income tax" are repudiated as a transgression against the teachings of Jesus on the question of property. Forgetting the theological significance of the story of the laborers in the vineyard (Matt. 20:1-16) one writer used it to underscore the premise that a man has a right to his own property. From the parable of the ten pounds (Luke 19:11-28) he derives the thought: "Not only did Jesus not believe in stealing, he did not believe that wealth was static."[27]

All the admonitions about covetousness in the New Testament would seem to presuppose the legitimacy of private property, but it must be understood that any claim for absolute property rights is excluded. From a Christian standpoint there is no such thing as "independent wealth." Man is only a steward who holds God's possessions in trust while waiting for the kingdom of God to be in-

[27] Cf. *Human Events* (December 22, 1961).

augurated. Jesus can scarcely be regarded as the defender of the propertied classes. The scribes are indicted for devouring widows' houses (Mark 12:40), and the Pharisees for practicing extortion. The summons to discipleship is a call to self-sacrifice which includes a readiness to renounce private possessions (cf. the encounter with the rich young ruler in Matt. 19). Noteworthy is the fact that Jesus and the Twelve met their day by day expenses from a common treasury. They were not interested in property values. As for himself, Jesus remarked: "Foxes have holes, and birds of the air have nests; but the Son of man has nowhere to lay his head" (Matt. 8:20). In the primordial Christian community in Jerusalem, human needs took precedence over property rights. Confronted by destitution and privation the early Christians voluntarily surrendered their personal possessions and distribution was made according to individual need.

Calling attention to these biblical precedents does not demand the abolition of private property or argue for the imposition of "Christian Socialism," but it does demonstrate incontrovertibly that it is a distortion of the prophetic and apostolic tradition to label "fair housing" ordinances immoral. Christians should be cautioned about protesting the invasion of the "sacred domain of private property" by legislation now pending in American cities and states that would seek to assure minorities of an equal opportunity to procure homes or rent rooms.

In Berkeley the fear was expressed that if the proposed ordinance was not defeated, home owners could be compelled to sell to "uncivilized" people of another race or apartments would have to be rented to men or women whose living habits might be objectionable. Actually the provisions of the ordinance contained ample safeguards against all conceivable abuses and would make it extremely unlikely that any unjustified charge of discrimination could be sustained. But for the Christian this should not be a decisive point. Even if the allegation were accurate that the enforcement of "fair housing" would result in isolated instances of false accusations against property holders, the Christian would still be obliged to raise the question of which is the greater menace to human welfare—the known reality of discrimination against minorities in housing that perpetuates degradation and suppression, or the theoretical possibility that a few innocent people might be wrongly accused along with those actually guilty of violating the enacted legislation.

The other deterrent to Christian support for fair housing seems to be the assumption that it is objectionable and unchristian to compel some citizens to treat other citizens honestly and equitably. The truism is quoted that "you cannot legislate righteousness." No verbal edict, it is argued, will automatically eradicate prejudice. You cannot create good will among the races by exerting force.

There is, of course, a degree of truth to these assertions. Police power and legal coercion in themselves will not guarantee that Negroes and whites will live side by side in harmony. The Christian gospel is the strongest liberating influence that we have at our disposal. When man is no longer separated from God he can use the power God conveys to him to break down the wall of hostility that alienates him from people who look or act differently from him. Nothing that sociologists or secular humanists project in their analyses and recommendations can lay bare our racial pride and shame our divisiveness so poignantly as the cross of Christ. The sacrificial death of God's Son for the reconciliation of man reduces all differences of class and color to insignificance. The intervention of the Spirit of God can convert a race-baiter into a lover of Negro slum dwellers and "white trash." Wherever the message of a God-given "peace on earth" is proclaimed and applied, racial discord may be overcome and more favorable relations among people may ensue. Correspondingly, Christian teaching can be an effective aid in eradicating ignorance and superstition about racial myths.

Pietists with their tradition of submission to authority and abhorrence of violence in any form have usually preferred to allow injustice to prevail unrebuked rather than sanction or encourage any remedy that would produce a social disturbance. Accordingly many

Christians have been critical of the career of Martin Luther King from the Montgomery bus boycott through the freedom riders and sit-ins to the 1965 voting drive in Selma. Negro leaders, they insist, should be more cautious and patient. Rather than being grateful for Christian Negro leadership which has advocated non-violent pressure and passive non-resistance that avert bloodshed, they resent any tactics that imply compulsion and accelerate the pace of change. Pious-minded Christians are often aghast at news reports that some clergymen, white and Negro, are breaking the law and being confined in jail. Somehow we seem to have neglected to develop a "theology of force" or a Christian social ethic that would allow for the appropriate implementation of judicial decisions and governmental power to gain the highest level of social justice attainable in an unjust world.

All of this became disturbingly evident in the Christian reluctance to support "fair housing" because it is "forcing the issue."

What many Christians forget when they are so sensitive about the use of legal devices and force to compel obedience to civil rights legislation, is that force is already being exerted by the segregationist or exploiter to bolster his prejudice or preserve his ill-gotten aggrandizement. There can be no doubt that force has been and will continue to be used. The only meaningful question is whether force will be used for *good* or for *evil.* If it is not employed to elevate the Negro to first class citizenship with the freedom to choose his own area of residence, it will be to "keep him in his place." What are unofficial "housing covenants" and all of the disguised and overt obstacles encountered by the Negro desiring decent housing in a stable neighborhood, but a morally reprehensible use of force? Again, the choice is between the enforcement of "fair housing" which might include the extremely remote possibility of a white person being falsely accused of discrimination, or the prolongation of the status quo which *forcibly* prevents Negroes from acquiring places of residence to which they would be entitled if equality were a reality.

"Righteous indignation" among Christians unfavorable to fair housing on the supposition that they are defending the sanctity of private property or endeavoring to promote better race relations through education and persuasion rather than compulsion must be dismissed as either an illusion based on misunderstanding or a rationalization assuaging a bad conscience.

What remains to be specified are some explicit and constructive recommendations as to what concerned Christians can do to cope with the housing problem for minorities. One thing is sure: if progress is to be made, the Christian church must renounce and eradicate its present mood of timidity and caution. The inviolability of private property and "peace at any price" must not be extolled as the supreme values. President Kennedy's executive order of November, 1962, barring discrimination in federally assisted housing, should have been a stimulus to the church. Robert C. Weaver, administrator of the Housing and Home Finance Agency, in a report on the first year following the late President's anti-bias order, predicted that 1964 would see the start of a significant dispersion of Negro families from "the segregated ghetto into the general community."[28] To move toward a real balance in social and economic affairs it may even be necessary to display a "positive discrimination" in favor of the Negro. Aggressive, unrelenting, and multi-pronged efforts will be indispensable: 1) Let prejudice itself be exposed as the sinister villain and attacked on every conceivable level, legal and educational. 2) Induce church leaders and church members to support and participate in every movement—local, regional, or national—which promises in our best judgment (without necessarily being perfect or ideal) to alleviate the distress of our colored brethren or other abused elements of the population—especially voluntary, sacrificial, nonviolent efforts on a nonpartisan basis. 3) Give full endorsement to fair housing legislation by states and cities throughout the country, not omitting or rejecting effective en-

[28] *Globe-Democrat* (St. Louis), AP report, December 11, 1963, p. 2*a*.

forcement procedures. 4) Devise more methods for closing the economic gap between Negro and white incomes. 5) Speak and act in behalf of a more extensive housing supply that is within the means of the people who are desperately in need. 6) Urge better understanding and more active cooperation from the real estate industry. 7) Call upon Christians everywhere to take the lead in announcing their willingness to accept full residential integration. 8) Dramatize to church groups and the community as a whole the inequalities in housing opportunities, the perils of segregation, the economic waste, and the social evils that ensue.

Donald S. Frey, an Evanston, Illinois, attorney, concludes:

> The Christian should see in the challenge to achieve the unity of mankind in the housing field an opportunity to become his full self as a Christian. He should persistently struggle for the unity of all men, calmly but firmly requesting equal treatment for himself and his fellow men. It is not enough for the White Christian to be prepared to accept his nonwhite neighbor into his community. He must love his neighbor to the point of bringing him in, of meeting and socializing with him, of living with him in truly integrated community. Man cannot live in freedom and truth unless his neighbor is able also to live in freedom and truth.[29]

[29] Donald S. Frey, "Christian Strategies in Housing," *Christian Century* (January 16, 1963). Copyright 1963 Christian Century Foundation. Reprinted by permission.

10 The Unfinished Task

An epochal event which rocked the South was the 1954 edict of the Supreme Court calling for the desegregation of public schools "with all deliberate speed." Some of the border states slowly began to comply, but in the Deep South a massive core of resistance was formed. Emancipation was to be deferred until some future generation. In fact, some zealots for segregation were determined to keep the Negro in an incessant state of social and economic inferiority. The southern way of life must never be abrogated. What is this way of life? John Bartlow Martin has described it as "the seamless garment of apartness . . . a black and white thread woven into the fabric of Southern life—its social, political, sexual, cultural, economic life." "This separation of the races," he says, "is like a vine which, rooted in slavery, never uprooted but merely twisted by the Civil War, flourished and by now entangles everyone and everything in a suffocating net from which no one, white or black, knows how to extricate himself."[1]

By 1963 more cracks had been made in the impregnable (?) wall of southern opposition, but racist politicians like Governor George C. Wallace continued to rave about federal interference and vowed to uphold "segregation now . . . segregation tomorrow . . . segregation forever." The past clung hard at the beginning of the

[1] John Bartlow Martin, *The Deep South Says Never* (New York: Ballantine, 1957), p. 7.

centennial year as Negroes were turned away from seven white churches in Albany, Georgia. Negotiations to desegregate four counties in Alabama, Mississippi, and Louisiana where some 35,000 children of United States military personnel go to school proved futile, and the Justice Department had to intervene directly.[2] Northern clergy and laity who had been imprisoned for a peaceful demonstration in support of the Albany movement[3] were put on trial and pronounced guilty.

Emancipation was far from complete as long as such absurdities could continue. As the NAACP put it on the eve of the centennial year:

> So long as black citizens are shot down, their churches burned, their livelihoods ended because they want to cast a ballot, Emancipation is not finished. So long as Negro children are denied the educational opportunity which is their birthright—be they in the North or in the South—Emancipation is not finished. Wherever and whenever the color of his skin keeps an American from buying the home of his choice or getting the job he needs or eating the meal he is ready to pay for, Emancipation is not finished.[4]

Slavery and racial injustice have been the great evils in American history which must perennially disturb the Christian conscience. Supposedly the Civil War defeated the slaveocracy, and the Fourteenth Amendment to the United States Constitution secured basic human rights for all of our citizens. Unfortunately the process of implementing our ideals has been painfully and disappointingly slow. Southerners as well as northerners were relieved when the curse of slavery was eradicated. But on both sides of the Mason and Dixon line white people have been largely indifferent as to the fate of the freed slaves, and their descendants. We have been re-

[2] *Newsweek* (January 28, 1963), p. 32.

[3] Desegregation efforts in Albany, Georgia, were stymied, and Martin Luther King had appealed to northern sympathizers to support the Negroes with their own presence.

[4] Quoted in *The Vanguard,* X (April, 1963), 6.

luctant to recognize the implications of our previous actions. We have postponed granting democratic rights to our neighbors of another color. And so a substantial number of Americans have continued to conform with the mores of segregation and to procrastinate in responding to the pleas of minorities. Many Christians, sometimes out of malice or fear, have hesitated to become personally involved in the renewed drive for freedom.

Notwithstanding, the social transformation is advancing. More progress toward real emancipation has been discernible in the last decade than in the preceding nine decades. All the while, the urge for equal dignity and opportunity is motivating the Negroes to exhibit an amazing vigor and to use promising new forms of action to reach their goals.

But much remains to be done before the "justice for all" affirmed in every pledge of allegiance to the American flag becomes a reality. By law or custom or the use of intimidation, in all sectors of our land, Negroes are still denied equal access to decent housing, good jobs, fair remuneration, recreational facilities, and educational opportunities. By 1962, eight years after the desegregation decision of the Supreme Court, only seven percent of Negro children in the South attended integrated schools. Despite all the pious resolutions of church conventions, eleven o'clock on Sunday morning continues to be the most segregated hour of the week. Because of their racial identity, Negroes live in constant danger of police brutality. In the South, even though there has been improvement in some places, they cannot be assured of impartial judgment when they stand before the bar. As long as these disabilities are not removed we cannot say that emancipation has been achieved.

Chester Bowles has offered a citizen's "checklist" which could serve as a kind of inventory for anyone who wants to examine his own community. By way of recapitulation it may be helpful to look at the series of inquiries he proposes:

> How many Negroes are members of the police force? The fire department? City Hall? The school system?

> Do Negroes have a full opportunity to get such jobs? And if so, are they promoted solely on merit and performance? What kind of housing, both public and private, is available to Negroes? What kind of medical and hospital care?
>
> Is there direct or indirect discrimination in public housing and entertainment facilities? What about the local barbershops and restaurants?
>
> What about private enterprise jobs? Are Negro workers given jobs which use their skills to the fullest?
>
> Is vocational and professional training freely available to qualified Negroes?
>
> Are the police and courts as fair to them as to other sections of the population?[5]

As the centennial observance of the Emancipation Proclamation came to a close the Protestants and Roman Catholics of America could not pretend to have purged themselves clean of all bias and discriminatory practices. Not all of the churches had crossed the racial barrier in requiring fair employment policies within their own institutions. Embarrassingly enough, after beating the drums for over a decade about aspiring toward a "nonsegregated church in a nonsegregated society," it could still be pointed out that less than five percent of the nation's Negro Protestants were affiliated with predominantly white denominations. That "kneel-ins" have to be staged to gain admission to houses of worship seems incredible. To see pictures of Negroes being arrested for entering white churches is utterly disgraceful. "Self-respect" will prevent the Negro from bruising "his knuckles perpetually on doors that white America refuses to open."[6]

To avoid the stigma of racism some churches have eagerly embraced token integration. Uneasy consciences have been appeased,

[5] Chester Bowles, "A Century Later: The New Commitment," *Saturday Review* (April 13, 1963).

[6] Gayraud S. Wilmore, Jr., "The New Negro and the Church," *Christian Century* (February 6, 1963), p. 170.

and white members have taken an intense pride in the presence of a few Orientals or a handful of Negroes in their assembled congregations. But these gestures of goodwill cannot be applauded enthusiastically. In most instances they must be dismissed as "too little and too late." If they are not accompanied by an aggressive unrestricted evangelism effort among *all* the people living in the environs of the church, and if they are not combined with a willingness to endorse open housing and join the struggle for social justice, these forms of limited integration will remain under the suspicion of hypocrisy and the condemnation of inadequacy.

Christian churches cannot claim to have attained emancipation in their own midst until de facto inclusiveness prevails everywhere. As long as the pigmentation of anyone's skin is a criterion for acceptance or rejection in any congregation, so long must the sin of racial arrogance be rebuked, and the Christian conscience be prodded. But as Gayraud S. Wilmore, Jr. has reminded us, much more must be done to renovate the church. Up to now, the Negro in revolt has an "impression of the white Protestant as at best a condescending, paternalistic gradualist." At worst he is a white supremacist who uses the Bible to "prove" that Negroes should be subservient to their masters and looks to his church as the last bastion of segregation. To erase this contemptible image Protestantism must somehow liberate itself from its captivity to "middle class white society" and align itself with the forces of revolution which are dedicated to full freedom for the oppressed peoples of the world. Unless this is done promptly and unequivocally we are likely to experience a further estrangement between Negro Christians and the white Christian community.[7]

Of course, predictions about the future of race relations in America are hazardous. No white man (or Negro?) can claim to have an intimate knowledge of the "Negro mentality." International events or economic crises could alter the situation unexpectedly and

[7] Cf. *ibid.*

accelerate or slacken developments which are presently discernible. Any analyses offered in the midst of a revolution could be subject to sudden change or modification.

With these admissions and cautionings in mind, however, it may be well to proceed to alert Christians to what may be anticipated as a result of the Negro revolt. Some of the prior assumptions of well-meaning Christians may have to be discarded.

In the future Negroes striving for their rights are not likely to wait for benevolent whites to set the strategy or timetable for specific actions to be undertaken. As it stands now, whites cannot expect to devise the plans or choose the objectives in what they might judge to be the wisest and safest course to pursue. Increasingly Negroes may be expected to set the pace and make the decisions. Throughout 1964 many Negroes manifested impatience, if not disdain, for white "liberal" leadership. Exasperated over what they judge to be paltry concessions grudgingly conceded, they have become distrustful. This does not excuse white Christians from becoming involved in the struggle for justice, but it does change the role which they have to perform.

In the days ahead we should not be surprised to find an excessive racial consciousness among some of the Negro people. No longer do they feel dependent upon the good will of white benefactors to improve their lot. Vigorous black leadership has inspired them with a new sense of pride and confidence. The crumbs that fall from the white man's table are not enough to appease their aroused appetites. Many Negroes are skeptical about the intentions and motivations of white collaborators. They may become unduly sensitive about race, and even be inclined to blame racial bias for untoward incidents which have nothing to do with the color of their skin. They may press demands which seem exorbitant. In all this the white man can scarcely complain. He is only reaping what he has sown. For generations members of the majority race in America have not only made the colored people the victims of their greed and hate; they have impressed upon them the notion that they are visibly and unalterably different. If the Negro is all too aware of his racial identity—if Black Muslims arise to emphasize racial purity and claim superiority—it is a reaction to indoctrination instilled by the white man.

Accordingly, we may expect Negro leaders to display the same kind of intransigence from which they have suffered. If men like Martin Luther King and Philip Randolph want to retain the respect of their people they cannot be content with negotiating compromises. The current mood of Negroes requires more drastic action and rapid change. Civil rights legislation which is "watered down" to conform with political realities is not likely to satisfy a minority which now wants to throw off completely the yoke of oppression it has so long endured.

It should not come as a surprise to us when Negroes resent criticism. Privately they may be "fed up" with the shenanigans of Adam Clayton Powell, but they may still object to hearing whites censure the immorality of a Negro politician when they have never protested the disgraceful antics of Governor Wallace or Senator Eastman. Corruption in government or conduct unbecoming a public servant cannot be ignored to spare Negro embarrassment, but caution should be exerted and the psychological response understood. There will long be those whites who are all too eager to expose instances of Negro malfeasance in high places. Only when one has erased the color boundary completely in his own thinking can he be free and unreserved in his critique of Negroes.

White people must admit that they cannot fully identify themselves with the Negro in his anguish. Christians should certainly seek to share the burdens of thier colored neighbors. Despite the best intentions, however, they cannot really comprehend what it means to be born and to live as a Negro. They cannot possibly feel the pain of segregation and the humiliation involved in being denied a meal and lodging because of one's color. No one should pretend, therefore, that he can speak with absolute appreciation for the Negro's point of view.

Christians should be on their guard against oversimplifications of the complexities confronting us in the race question. Discrimination in employment is reprehensible and should be eliminated wherever possible. But grave economic problems may frustrate this objective. More jobs to overcome unemployment in general will help alleviate the distress of both races. A war on poverty, overcoming some of the disadvantages handicapping underprivileged people everywhere, will brighten the prospect for Negroes. Transmitting the skills required in modern industry, averting school dropouts, and motivating Negro youngsters to exert greater effort are all part of the total program that is required to assure improvement.

Also, broad generalizations about the Negro are dubious. Whatever is said about "the Negro character" or the intentions of "the new Negro" has to be taken with the proverbial grain of salt. As individuals, Negroes differ greatly in temperament and attitude. Some may become fiercely angry. Others will remain stolidly apathetic. And there will be many somewhere in between.[8]

There may always be a time for moderation, properly understood and properly applied. Hot-heads and sensationalists are scarcely a credit to a crusade for Negro emancipation. Screaming about the barbarities of slavery only inflamed the passions of men and women, without necessarily inducing them to take concrete steps toward its eradication. Fulminating about the evils of segregation may only gain one notoriety as a fanatic without improving the lot of the Negro in the least.

The erroneous conclusion sometimes follows that Christians should steer clear of any acts that might be construed as agitation. Moderation is esteemed as the highest virtue and becomes an impressive rationalization for staying on the sidelines while others "sit in" at lunch counters, face hostile crowds, or go to prison. No real

[8] Some of the foregoing thoughts were suggested by Roger L. Shinn in his article "Axioms for White Liberals," *Christianity and Crisis*, XXIII (September 30, 1963), 167.

distinction is made between belligerent extremists and the advocates of nonviolence. According to a *Newsweek* poll taken in the fall of 1963, white Americans by a margin of two to one complained that Negroes are moving "too fast."

Probably the most cogent rebuttal to this untenable type of "moderation" ever written came in Martin Luther King's celebrated and eloquent "Letter from Birmingham Jail." Eight clergymen had issued a statement calling his demonstration in the Alabama metropolis "unwise and untimely." Patience and negotiation were advocated as preferable to direct action.

King's response pierced the conscience of many white Christians:

> For years now I have heard the word "Wait!" . . . This "Wait" has almost always meant "Never." . . . We have waited for more than 340 years for our constitutional and God-given rights. . . . Perhaps it is easy for those who have never felt the stinging darts of segregation to say "Wait." But when you have seen vicious mobs lynch your mothers and fathers at will, and drown your sisters and brothers at whim; when you have seen hate-filled policemen curse, kick and even kill your black brothers and sisters with impunity; when you see the vast majority of your 20 million Negro brothers smothering in an air-tight cage of poverty in the midst of an affluent society; when you suddenly seek to explain to your six-year-old daughter why she can't go to the public amusement park that has just been advertised on television . . . when you have to concoct an answer for a five-year-old son asking "Daddy, why do white people treat colored people so mean?"; when you take a cross-country drive and find it necessary to sleep night after night in the uncomfortable corners of your automobile because no motel will accept you; when you are humiliated day in and day out by nagging signs reading "white" and "colored"; when your first name becomes "nigger," your middle name becomes "boy" (however old you are), . . . and your wife and mother are never given the respected title "Mrs."; when you are harried by day and haunted by night by the fact that you are a Negro; . . . and are plagued with inner fears and outer resentments; when you are forever fighting a degenerate sense of "nobodiness"—then you will understand why we find it difficult to wait. There comes a time when the cup of endurance runs over, and men are no longer

willing to be plunged into an abyss of injustice where they experience the bleakness of corroding despair. . . ."[9]

Gradualists of Christian persuasion have often objected to the breaking of laws by the "abolitionists" of the 1960's. Integration enthusiasts call for compliance with the rulings of the Supreme Court which outlaw segregation, while assuming the prerogative of disobeying statutes which still require the separation of the races. Is this not inconsistent and illegitimate? Dr. King replies by quoting St. Augustine's judgment that "an unjust law is no law at all" and elaborates:

> An unjust law is a code that is out of harmony with the moral law. . . . All segregation statutes are unjust. . . . Segregation . . . substitutes an "I-it" relationship for an "I-thou" relationship and ends up relegating persons to the status of things. Hence segregation is not only politically, economically and sociologically unsound, it is sinful.[10]

King makes it clear that he does not endorse disrespect for law and order that could lead to anarchy. "One who breaks an unjust law," he cautions, "must do so *openly, lovingly* [emphases his], and with a willingness to accept the penalty." Arousing the conscience of the community over the detrimental effects of bad laws, he maintains, "is in reality expressing the highest respect for law."

Civil disobedience, King recalls, is not something novel which he invented. "It was evidenced sublimely in the refusal of Shadrach, Meshach, and Abednego to obey the laws of Nebuchadnezzar, on the ground that a higher moral law was at stake." The early Christian martyrs were thrown to the lions because they defied the decrees of the Roman emperor. To clinch his argument the intrepid leader of the Negro revolt reminds those who insists that Christians must always be law abiding citizens that it was an offense against the established regime to offer aid and comfort to a Jew during the

[9] Martin Luther King, Jr., "Letter from Birmingham Jail," *Christian Century* (June 12, 1963). Copyright 1963 Christian Century Foundation. Reprinted by permission.

[10] *Ibid.*

Nazi era, and in 1956 it was "illegal" to join the Hungarian freedom fighters. Obviously, blind submission to tyranny is not the best way to exercise Christian responsibility.[11]

Nothing has been more pathetic than the failure of the self-styled moderates to make any impact in overcoming the racial evils that beset our society. They have been frozen with uncertainty and inaction. When the debacle in Birmingham was at its lowest depth of degradation in the spring of 1963, a reporter for the San Francisco *Chronicle* made a special investigation of all the white churches in the area. What were they doing when the crisis was at its height to offer guidance or to stimulate their members to rise above hatred and spread reconciliation? The critique of the reporter was devastating, for the white churches of Birmingham were paralyzed with fear and contributed absolutely nothing to the "peace of the city."

No wonder that Martin Luther King is exasperated over the conduct of white moderates who only block social progress with their shallow grasp of the real situation. Men of good will who want to proceed slowly and avoid conflict are forgetting that tensions and violence already exist in the outrages that whites perpetrate against Negroes with impunity. "I had hoped," laments King, "that the white moderate would understand that the present tension in the South is a necessary phase of the transition from an obnoxious negative peace, in which the Negro passively accepted his unjust plight, to a substantive and positive peace, in which all men will respect the dignity and worth of human personality." After initial disappointment at being labeled an "extremist" he is prepared to wear the designation as a badge of honor for he finds that Amos, Paul, Luther, and many other men of God were denounced as agitators long before he appeared on the scene.[12]

[11] Cf. Martin Luther King, *Why We Can't Wait* (New York: Harper, 1964).
[12] King, "Letter from Birmingham Jail."

As many predicted, the racial crisis took an ominous turn in 1964. Doubts were expressed that cool-headed Negro leaders would be able to restrain the rising tide of anger. The nonviolent approach of Martin Luther King was repudiated as ineffective by men who clamored for immediate results and were prepared to resort to forcible means if their demands were turned down. Agreeing that "we can't wait" the new militants stirred up a fiery resentment that threatened to erupt in violence almost anywhere at any time.

As a worried government awaited the "long, hot summer of discontent" storm signals arose in Mississippi. A wide cross section of American youth, inspired by the ideal of freedom for suppressed Negroes, volunteered to "invade" the most segregated state to help register voters. As hundreds of civil rights campaigners poured into Mississippi, three disappeared. Their station wagon was found burned. After a prolonged and dreary search through the swamplands by sailors, and an intensive investigation by FBI agents, the bodies of the murdered victims were recovered. Other terroristic activities broke out. A number of Negro churches were burned and homes were damaged by dynamite explosions.

Then the racial cauldron boiled over in the cities of the North. The spark was ignited in Harlem when an off-duty white police lieutenant killed a fifteen-year-old Negro boy in a sidewalk free-for-all tussle. A menacing crowd marched on the police station hooting: "Killer cops! Murderers!" The more the officers tried to disperse the demonstrators the more vehement they became. Soon central Harlem was aflame with raging hatred. Rioters plunged madly through the streets. Rocks, bricks, and garbage can lids were hurled at the police. Bottles rained down from tenement rooftops. Molotov cocktails burst in sheets of flame. Looters smashed store windows and escaped with armloads of booty. A Black Nationalist bookstore ornamented with a picture of a black Jesus and a sign reading "God Dam White Man" was set ablaze. Police fought back with night sticks and sent crackling volleys of revolver fire into the air. But every bullet and every bloodied head was a new incitement to mob violence. Rumors of police atrocities spread and caused even more frenzy. Jesse Gray, the firebrand Harlem rent-strike leader, was reported to have drawn cheers when he cried out for "guerrilla warfare" and for "100 skilled black revolutionaries who are ready to die." Peace appeals fell on deaf ears, and before the rioting had completely subsided in Harlem it leaped across the East River to a tumble-down section of Brooklyn. At the end of the tumultuous week a bloody conflict burst out in Rochester, New York, and rumblings of discontent were heard in many other northern urban centers.

In an interview with the West German news magazine *Der Spiegel,* James Baldwin bluntly asserted that the United States might be on the verge of a civil war between blacks and whites unless the government intervened vigorously in behalf of social justice. Baldwin belittled the civil rights achievements of the justice department and referred to Harlem's ghetto as a "concentration camp." Openly exclaiming that "the fire has started" he feared that "the turning point may be disaster."[13]

Some evidence was accumulated to suggest that professional agitators had assumed leading roles in the racial riots. Extremists—communists and Black Muslims—were accused of stoking the flames of anger as high as they could. Organized gangs obviously took advantage of the disorders as a convenient cover for pilferage.

Nevertheless, it was undeniable that the explosions in northern cities would not have occurred if there had not been long-standing grievances that had embittered the Negro communities. The pleas and warnings of Negro spokesmen and their white collaborators had gone unheeded. How could Harlem's residents be content when their unemployment rate was double the white man's, when one Negro man out of four was out of work, and average annual earnings were almost two thousand dollars less than that of white families? The social sores that fester in Harlem breed cynicism and

[13] Cf. "Baldwin: U. S. Near Unavoidable Bloodbath," *Examiner* (San Francisco), July 27, 1964.

despair. Half of the families are reputed to be splintered with all the detrimental effects this domestic chaos imposes upon the children. Kids lag behind in their ghetto schools and are tempted to drop out. Many of the houses in Harlem are delapidated, overcrowded, and rat infested. A quarter of a million people are jammed into three and one-half square miles. Absentee landlords charge exorbitant rents. Under such adverse conditions crime flourishes. Harlem's homicide rate is six times as high as the rest of New York City, its juvenile delinquency twice as high, its narcotics rate ten times as high.[14]

Notwithstanding the dehumanizing squalor and congestion that evoke misery and violence in a place like Harlem, many white Christians are inclined to seek a remedy solely in terms of punishment for lawlessness. Overlooking the multitude of legitimate complaints that have gone unredressed in the Negro ghettoes for decades, they consider the rioting *only* as a crime problem to be eradicated by reinforcing the police and imposing stiffer penalties on those who disturb the peace. With presidential aspirants promising to gain respect for law and order, and with Polish and Italian minorities frightened by Negro competition for their jobs and encroachments on their living space, there was widespread talk about a "white backlash" that could block further advances on the civil rights front. Irish immigrants and every other minority group, it is argued, struggled long for a hard-earned place in the sun. Negroes, it is presumed, are expecting too much too fast. Whites who are tired of hearing Negroes press their demands believe that they have found a rationale for "holding them back." Even "church people" have felt justified in rebuking the Negro drive for equality. That racial prejudice is by no means confined to the South became shockingly evident when Governor Wallace of Alabama garnered sizeable chunks of the vote in presidential primaries in Wisconsin, Indiana, and Maryland.

The type of perverted thinking that was poisoning the "white

[14] Cf. *Newsweek* (August 3, 1964).

backlash" can be found in a release of the Congress of Racial Intellect entitled "15 Questions on Integration." Some samples:

> Why is the Negro still a cannibal and headhunter in New Guinea? . . . Why has he never learned in some parts of the world to count higher than 3? . . . Why has he never followed the pattern of the Chinese and Mormons who built their own cities and businesses? . . . Why does the white man owe the Negro employment at the expense of firing of his own kind? . . . Why have thousands of deprived white people overcome lack of education and poverty and gone on to invent the airplane and countless thousands of inventions that make possible our competitive markets abroad? . . . Why should anybody be forced to hire, associate with, marry, dance, or live with anybody they do not wish to? . . . Why is the Negro crime rate so high that integrationists are ashamed to discuss it? . . .[15]

Here, once again (this time for distribution among northern bigots) are repeated *ad nauseam* the stale stereotypes and misleading half-truths that have fostered racial antipathies for over a century. Untenable and oft-refuted myths are brazenly revived. The past performance of the Negro is harshly judged on the basis of western European standards of excellence, and with a total disregard for the stigma of slavery which has been attached to the Negro in a degrading way that no other race or nationality in the United States has endured. As usual, the Negro quest for equal privileges and opportunities is confused with the implication that what this underdog surreptitiously craves is an intimate personal association that will somehow abrogate one's personal right to choose his own friends and marriage partner. Negroes are blamed for the high incidence of crime in their ranks, but nothing is said about the corrupt environment by which they are encircled or the lack of incentive for honesty and respectability when people are frustrated by deprivation.

Actually it is a marvel that Negroes have not rebelled *more*

[15] Excerpts from "15 Questions on Integration." In the possession of the writer.

against law enforcement agencies than they have. Unfair treatment before the bar of justice and police brutality have been commonplace in their experience. In recent years the Inter-Citizens Committee of Birmingham, Alabama, has gathered sworn testimony covering innumerable instances of cruelty and physical injury inflicted upon Negroes by whites who have been entrusted with upholding the law. Time and again trivial offenses have served as excuses for extreme malice and inhumane beatings. Even those black citizens who have violated no law at all can be confronted with "trumped up" charges, maltreated, fined and imprisoned. Negroes who have not resisted arrest have been blinded or maimed for life by intoxicated officers who delighted in unmercifully browbeating their victims. Peaceful civil rights demonstrators have been seized and threatened. A Negro in Gadsden, Alabama, who spent three and a half years in the Army during World War II, and was honorably discharged, "felt the cattle prods and the billy sticks" after he joined his community's struggle for freedom. A Negro Navy veteran in the same city was struck in the genitals and was hospitalized with bruises.[16]

On the evening of May 24, 1964, James Eddie Steele, a Negro college student, was on his way to visit his girl friend at her home near the Bethel Baptist Church in Birmingham. Before he reached his destination he was abruptly stopped at an intersection by a police car. Denying the absurd accusation that he was driving ninety miles an hour, and refusing to sign the ticket handed him, young Steele was jerked out of his car, and though handcuffed and defenseless, was manhandled by two officers who took turns hitting him all over his body with their fists and a night stick. Infuriated by the screaming pleas of his mother they cursed him with "vile names" and warned him to "get out of town" after his trial. Given medical treatment at a hospital, he was "stuck" with all of the bills.

[16] Documents 55 and 56 on Human Rights in Alabama. Sworn testimony received on March 27 and March 31, 1964. Released by the Inter-Citizens Committee, Box 1443, Birmingham, Alabama, C. Herbert Oliver, Executive Secretary.

Tried and found guilty he was fined four hundred dollars plus costs, and given 360 days.[17]

On the night of September 4, 1963, following the second bombing of the home of attorney Arthur Shores, a twenty-year-old Negro youth who had just returned from two years service in the U. S. Army in Germany was shot twice in the base of the skull from behind, and once through the upper left arm and into the chest. Two days later the coroner ruled that John Coley was the victim of "stray pellets from a shotgun." An autopsy was performed and the bullets removed without the knowledge of his parents. The *Birmingham News* reported that police shot John Coley . . . "when he burst from a house firing a gun," but a close friend swore that he was unarmed. "The killing was wholly unnecessary" was the verdict of the Inter-Citizens Committee after they had investigated the case.[18]

Despite the denials of police commissioners, Negroes in the North frequently complained about acts of brutality. In Harlem the forces of "law and order" were mistrusted and viewed more like an army of occupation. Persistent rumors were heard about police complicity in such lucrative enterprises as the numbers game and the narcotics traffic. Reports of shakedowns and bribe-taking were too widespread to be dismissed as groundless falsehoods. The riots in Rochester were triggered by the arrest of a seventeen-year-old Negro on charges of public drunkenness. For many months there had been a smoldering bitterness over the vicious beating of another young Negro.[19]

[17] Document 68. Sworn testimony received on June 11, 1964. Cf. the Travis Case, Document 20, concerning which C. Herbert Oliver wrote on November 26, 1963: "The officers involved were tried and exonerated by an all white jury. Justice was non-existent and mercy was in hiding." (Letter on file.)

[18] Cf. *John Coley,* a brochure with pictures of the gun wounds. Issued by Inter-Citizens Committee.

[19] Cf. *Newsweek* (August 3, 1964): "[A Harlem housewife murmured:] The real criminal is the cops. They permit dope, numbers, whores, gangsters to operate here, and all the time they get money under the table—and I ain't talkin' about $2 neither." Cf. "A Racial Cauldron Boils Over," Editorial, *Christian Century* (August 5, 1964). Cf. William Stringfellow, *My People is the Enemy* (New York: Holt, Rinehart and Winston, 1964).

Obviously Christians cannot condone violence and vandalism. Tirelessly their search must continue for a peaceful solution to social ills. But this eagerness to avoid bloodshed must not be allowed to deteriorate into an irrelevant Christian piety that values serenity above all else. Too quickly and too uncritically church-affiliated people embrace "the powers that be" to compel the obedience of disgruntled groups. Too easily, complex problems are circumvented by the assumption that if only the criminials are apprehended with stiffer penalties and the laws enforced more rigorously all will be well. And such self-acclaimed Christians can exult in their own righteousness as they undergird the white backlash.

The earlier stages of the Negro revolt which were characterized by a disciplined, nonviolent approach were more palatable to fastidious Christians than the later battles in which bricks have been thrown and the ugliness of desperate conflict has marred our idealism. But it is precisely at this point that the crucial test is arising for the Christian conscience. Can this conscience find its way through the labyrinth of perplexing moral enigmas and difficult concrete decisions that have to be made in the days ahead if the goal of Negro emancipation is not to be forfeited? Can it resist the temptation to become aligned with reactionary forces operating under the guise of defending constitutional liberties and states rights? Or even more vexing to the delicate conscience, can it avert the suppressing of just demands of minorities when social stability appears to be menaced by the way these demands are pressed?

Certainly the year 1964 recorded greater advances by the churches in better race relations than they had ever made before. Protestant denominations and Catholic bishops issued bolder and more pointed pronouncements against segregation than their constituents had previously heard. The United Church of Christ filed a petition with the Federal Communications Commission asking that license renewal be denied to two Jackson, Mississippi, television stations on the ground that they practice racial discrimination.[20]

[20] Cf. *Christian Century* (June 3, 1964).

In staid New England the same denomination ruffled some independent-minded congregations which are reluctant to open their doors to non-whites or accept Negro clergy as their pastors. At least some suburban parishes acted courageously to refute the cynics who say that the churches will inevitably bend their principles to conform with their institutional interests. Threatened by a financial boycott that caused a decline of about twenty-five percent in its income in 1964, a suburban congregation in Chicago continued to insist upon preparing the membership for the reception of races other than their own.[21]

Bishop Joseph Gomez of the African Methodist Episcopal Church (Negro) commended the National Council of Churches for its forthright stand in favor of the civil rights bill. Members of Congress were flooded with mail from churchmen who urged prompt passage of the long-pending legislation. Significantly, Senator Richard Russell of Georgia blamed the clergy of the nation for contributing to the defeat of the southern filibuster by making civil rights a moral issue.

Through its Commission on Religion and Race the National Council of Churches collaborated in the training of over one thousand student volunteers for participation in the Mississippi Summer Project. Preparing to live in Negro homes and help Negroes to vote, this cross-section of American youth remained undaunted by the news that three of their fellow workers had been brutally murdered. Knowing that they could expect harrassments, arrests, and burned crosses, and admitting that they were frightened, most of them persevered. Some of the young enthusiasts professed a Christian motivation for their sense of dedication to the cause. A senior coed from Southern Illinois University, a Lutheran, recalled that her pastor had spoken out against racial intolerance within her congregation. A girl from Davenport, Iowa, had gained her inspiration by working with the Catholic Interracial Council in her home community. The daughter of a Presbyterian minister from Decatur,

[21] *Ibid.* (August 12, 1964).

Illinois, admired her father who had been one of a hundred clergymen involved in the Hattiesburg, Mississippi, Freedom Day on January 22, 1964, when homes were canvassed, the county court house picketed, and mass rallies sponsored at the churches.[22] The crusading daughter of a Baptist minister, herself a native of Georgia, wrote from Mississippi to her parents in California that she would stay to attain freedom, no matter what perils arose. She was even ready "to die if necessary."[23]

The most hopeful achievement in 1964 was the bipartisan action which invoked cloture in the Senate to halt the talking marathon by southern obstructionists and to assure passage of the church-endorsed civil rights legislation. Among the most important provisions of the bill is the authority given to the Attorney General to initiate suits to desegregate public facilities and to intervene in school desegregation cases where the injured party is unable to pursue the legal remedies. Discrimination on the basis of race or religion is prohibited in hotels, motels, restaurants, theaters, and other public accommodations. Employers and labor unions whose operations affect interstate commerce and with twenty-five or more employees are forbidden to deny equal opportunity to all races. To protect the franchise in federal elections, the voting section of the law disallows differential applications of voting tests and the denial of registration because of minor errors in making application.

There can be no doubt that the civil rights bill represents a giant step forward in the drive for Negro equality, especially if it is energetically enforced. But implementation will be difficult if a growing favorable sentiment across the length and breadth of the land does not back up its provisions. Wherever possible it will be desirable to gain voluntary compliance with the law. The Republican candidate for the presidency in 1964, while avowedly not a racist, voted against the civil rights legislation with the objection that several of its provisions are unconstitutional. Notwithstanding his

[22] *The Vanguard* (May-June, 1964).
[23] *Chronicle* (San Francisco), July 28, 1964.

apparent personal integrity and good intentions, Senator Goldwater's stand gave encouragement to right wing extremists who denounced the law and announced their intention to defy it.

Here is where Christian witness can again be most helpful. While it may be necessary to continue protest movements and demonstrations to expose flagrant injustices, it will also be imperative to redouble our efforts to create a reservoir of good will and an improvement in interpersonal relations that will enable the races to live together in tranquility. Let Christians be urged to take the lead in fulfilling the intent behind the Civil Rights Act, and in moving beyond the letter of the law, to more than comply with what is absolutely required. Let them refute and silence by word and example the gainsayers, the hate mongers and the radical rightists. Let them bring a generous measure of Christian love into an expanding atmosphere of mutual understanding and peaceful transition.

An immense and incomplete task stares us in the face. The real test for the Christian church is still ahead. Complacency could easily obviate the gains that have been made. "The Church itself is not yet emancipated," a Negro bishop told an audience in Washington, D. C., shortly before the Civil Rights Acts was pushed through the Senate:

> We must meet and deal with the ever-present fear of some churches and ministers of offending certain strong and influential forces in their constituency. . . . The question before us is whether the Church dares to accept its Christlike role . . . even to the point of accepting the cross that such a role entails. The Church must be emancipated from all those methods of institutionalism that frustrate and hamper the work of God's kingdom. . . . The Christian must pray not that the struggle be made easy but that we shall have the strength to prosecute it to the fullest . . . that we refuse to be delivered from its pain but be buoyed by its promise—as we work for a united Church, a united ministry, and a united people.[24]

[24] News release of the Commission on Religion and Race, National Council of Churches, June 12, 1964.

Whites, no less than Negroes, need to experience an emancipation of mind and heart. The white moderates of the South who know that their past treatment of the Negro as a slave or as an inferior has been wrong, but who cannot speak out for fear of reprisals from the Ku Klux Klan or the White Citizens Councils must be liberated from their timidity. The white Christians of the North who are still self-satisfied or apathetic must be aroused to a keener sensitivity of their own guilt and then set free for redemptive action by their own personal encounter with the mercy exhibited in the incarnation and death of God's Son. Even the white backlash and the Black Nationalists must not be scorned as beyond all reclamation. Wherever the Spirit of God can permeate human lives with the promise of recovery and the message of hope centered in Jesus Christ, the impossible can become possible, full emancipation can become a reality.

Will we use the incomparable power that God has placed at our disposal? Who can doubt that if the Christian church had been the "salt of the earth" and the "light of the world" in renouncing slavery and racial antagonism, many of the gruesome events which stain the pages of human history could have been averted? If Christian leadership in our own country had taken a firm stand in behalf of justice for the Negro after the Civil War and up to the present, it could have made an appreciable difference in advancing the ex-slaves and integrating them into American society. If the church had set an example by becoming an authentic interracial community with its own members, it could have gone a long way toward healing the racial sickness around it. Christians, if they had emulated their heroic antecedents, would never have surrendered to Jim Crow laws or allowed their colored brethren to be trampled upon. There was a time when the church had the opportunity to make a significant contribution to resolving the nation's racial problems.

Alas! That time seems to be gone. Changes have come rapidly in the last few years promising liberation for the Negro. The long-delayed day of full emancipation from humiliation and abuse may be dawning. But not thanks to Christian intervention! When Dr. Herbert Blumer, Professor of Sociology and Criminology at the University of California in Berkeley, lectured to a public audience in the spring of 1963 on the gains that have been made by the Negro in the last sixty years and what further advances may be anticipated in the next generation, he flatly denied that Christian beliefs had anything at all to do with the improvement that has been witnessed. The thesis that Christians have helped by propagating good will across racial lines he discounted as fictitious. Sheer industrial growth, the combatting of discrimination in some labor unions, and especially direct governmental action have been some of the causative factors in expediting the rise of the Negro; but the churches score zero in Dr. Blumer's evaluation.

On July 29, 1963, while the Walther League (the youth organization of The Lutheran Church—Missouri Synod) was conducting its convention in Washington, D. C., Negro entertainer Dick Gregory was interviewed before thirty-five hundred young people. When asked if he thought the church was still a power that could do something to benefit the Negro, he startled the audience by replying:

> My personal conviction is I believe it's too late. . . . We had the Civil War and then 100 years later—it would have been a great thing had the Church stepped forward with leadership to free a great many of the oppressed people in America. This would have been a feather in God's cap. We would have said, "Thank God." The Church has failed in such a horrible way that now everyone seems to say, "Thank the Supreme Court."[25]

Indubitably the cynics have abundant reasons to cast aspersions at the institutional church for its colossal shortcomings in race relations. Christians have been weighed in the balances on this crucial

[25] Reported in *Arena* (November, 1963), p. 11.

issue and have been found deficient in love and courage.

But laws alone will not change the recalcitrant. The races will not live together in mutual respect and harmony under coercion. Sinful emotions will continue to dictate customs that are at variance with judicial decisions. To resolve the "American dilemma" the power of Christian proclamation and the example of Christ-inspired lives are sorely needed. The church has the means for restraining and transmuting the vagrant passions of men if it will only apply them to the worst malady that persists in our society. "God was in Christ reconciling the world to himself" (II Cor. 5:19), be reconciled to one another. "Let justice roll down like waters, and righteousness like an overflowing stream" (Amos 5:24). And there are signs that a troubled conscience is stirring the church. Here and there white voices are being raised against the menace of racism, even when it means jeopardizing their positions or endangering their lives.

Church resolutions on racial matters sometimes have not been much more than favorable publicity at a time when it is popular to endorse civil rights for minorities. One can hope, however, that with all of the fertile seeds being planted some will fall on good soil, take firm rootage, and produce abundant fruit. One cannot disregard as altogether futile the forthright resolution approved by the General Board of the National Council of Churches in the middle of 1963:

> The Church of Jesus Christ can make no compromise with discrimination against or segregation of peoples on the basis of race and still be faithful to her Master. God came to make His dwelling among men in the person of a man. He went to His death and rose again for every man.[26]

The spokesmen for the National Council regretfully admit that the church has grievously sinned, that many congregations still

[26] A partial text of the resolution promulgated on June 7, 1963 may be found in *Christianity and Crisis* (July 8, 1963).

close their doors to Negroes, that church institutions continue to discriminate against minorities, and that there has been too much "fumbling expediency" seen in a readiness to settle for "gradual change" and "modest tokens of progress."

The celerity of the revolution now demands that we "put aside every lesser engagement," confess our "sins of omission and delay," and enter into "costly action that may jeopardize the organizational goals and institutional structures of the Church, and may disrupt any fellowship that is less than fully obedient to the Lord of the Church."[27]

The unfinished task confronting Christians who are seriously involved in the second great crusade for Negro emancipation can perhaps be illustrated, as a final conclusion to this treatise, by referring to the experiences of sixty Yale students who went to Mississippi to work on the protest campaign for Aaron Henry, a Negro druggist, who ran unofficially for governor in the 1963 election. Kenneth Klotz, one of the participants, told about the mockery of justice which could have him arrested on the absurd charge of assault and battery, while another young man was accused of obstructing traffic with a Volkswagon and taken into custody on suspicion of auto theft (in spite of the fact that he produced his registration papers). Young Klotz, a Yale Senior, pondered the meaning of what had happened to him and its relation to the whole plight of the Negro:

> We can somehow sit back and occupy ourselves with our own personal, selfish concerns, completely divorced from this shame of our society. Our Christian conscience somehow manages to close its eyes when it is most needed. All that remains is the dogged perseverance and Christian love of the Negroes in their fight toward equality. Some day they really will overcome. . . . I cried tonight because I remembered the smiling, unconcerned faces of Negro youngsters who will never know a real educa-

[27] *Ibid.*

tion, playing in their segregated school yard; . . . because my letters to my congressmen will not make people treat a Negro like a human being unless millions of people change their attitude of apathy. My feeling after three days in Mississippi is one of disgust tinged with shock and frustration. . . . I am still a white agitator, and I will remain a white agitator until I am no longer ashamed to be called a Christian and an American.[28]

[28] Kenneth Klotz, "Mississippi: 1963," *Lutheran Layman* (December 1, 1963), p. 10.

Index